FOURTH EDITION

# Writing Papers in Psychology

## A STUDENT GUIDE

Ralph L. Rosnow
Temple University

Mimi Rosnow

Brooks/Cole Publishing Company

I(T)P® *An International Thomson Publishing Company*

Pacific Grove • Albany • Belmont • Bonn • Boston • Cincinnati • Detroit
Johannesburg • London • Madrid • Melbourne • Mexico City • New York • Paris
Singapore • Tokyo • Toronto • Washington

Sponsoring Editor: *Jim Brace-Thompson*
Marketing Team: *Romy Taormina, Lauren Harp, Alicia Barelli*
Marketing Representative: *Joyce Larcom*
Editorial Assistant: *Terry Thomas*
Production Editor: *Marjorie Z. Sanders*
Manuscript Editor: *Margaret Ritchie*

Permissions Editor: *Cathleen Collins Morrison*
Interior and Cover Design: *Laurie Albrecht*
Art Coordinator and Interior Illustration: *Lisa Torri*
Cover Photo: *Charles Daniels/Photonica*
Typesetting: *Bookends Typesetting*
Printing and Binding: *Edwards Brothers, Inc.*

*For more information, contact:*

BROOKS/COLE PUBLISHING COMPANY
511 Forest Lodge Road
Pacific Grove, CA 93950
USA

International Thomson Editores
Seneca 53
Col. Polanco
11560 México, D.F., México

International Thomson Publishing Europe
Berkshire House 168-173
High Holborn
London WC1V 7AA
England

International Thomson Publishing GmbH
Königswinterer Strasse 418
53227 Bonn
Germany

Thomas Nelson Australia
102 Dodds Street
South Melbourne, 3205
Victoria, Australia

International Thomson Publishing Asia
221 Henderson Road
#05-10 Henderson Building
Singapore 0315

Nelson Canada
1120 Birchmount Road
Scarborough, Ontario
Canada M1K 5G4

International Thomson Publishing Japan
Hirakawacho Kyowa Building, 3F
2-2-1 Hirakawacho
Chiyoda-ku, Tokyo 102
Japan

Printed in the United States of America

10  9  8  7  6  5  4  3  2

**Library of Congress Cataloging-in-Publication Data**

Rosnow, Ralph L.
    Writing papers in psychology : a student guide / Ralph L. Rosnow & Mimi Rosnow.—4th ed.
        p.  cm.
    Includes index.
    ISBN 0-534-34826-2
    1. Psychology—Authorship.   2. Report writing.   I. Rosnow, Mimi, 1938–  .  II. Title.
BF76.7.R67      1998
808'.06615—DC21
                                                            96-3844
                                                              CIP

# To the partnership
## that brought this book about

**Ralph L. Rosnow** is the Bolton Professor of Psychology at Temple University and has also taught at Boston University and Harvard University. He has written numerous books and journal articles on a wide variety of topics in psychology and related fields.

**Mimi Rosnow** took her undergraduate degree in English at Wheaton College in Norton, Massachusetts. She has done freelance editorial consulting and for a number of years was an editorial assistant at a national magazine.

# CONTENTS

# EXHIBITS

# PREFACE

*Writing Papers in Psychology* began as a student manual designed to teach specialized writing skills. In this fourth edition, we have updated the book's focus so that technological advances are given a greater emphasis. What started as a writing manual for students in psychology and related fields remains just that, but it also now incorporates a new chapter on drafting the proposal, a new sample essay and two new research reports (experimental and archival), ethical guidelines, and tips for using the new technology to be found in libraries.

Guided by the following flowchart, students can refer to specific chapters and sections as needed:

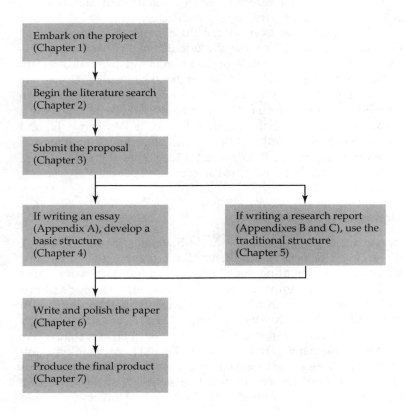

Embark on the project
(Chapter 1)

Begin the literature search
(Chapter 2)

Submit the proposal
(Chapter 3)

If writing an essay
(Appendix A), develop a
basic structure
(Chapter 4)

If writing a research report
(Appendixes B and C), use the
traditional structure
(Chapter 5)

Write and polish the paper
(Chapter 6)

Produce the final product
(Chapter 7)

## Recommended Style

The recommended style is close to that spelled out in the *Publication Manual of the American Psychological Association* (1994, 4th edition) but departs from the APA publication manual in a few respects. In the case of omissions or deviations, the rule of thumb that has guided us is utility, as the APA manual states that it "is not intended to cover scientific writing at an undergraduate level, because preferences for style at that level are diverse" (p. 332). *Writing Papers* is designed to provide accessible forms for that diversity in order to make the process of conceptualizing, writing, and producing a required paper both meaningful and palatable to students.

For example, we recommend that the introductory section have a center heading, whereas journal manuscripts omit it. We feel this heading will help to keep the student on course as a constant reminder of the purpose of this section. We are flexible about the placement of tables and figures, emphasizing readability rather than the technical requirements of compositors. Consistent with the APA publication manual, we recommend that letters used as statistical symbols or algebraic variables be underlined, but we say that formulaic symbols may be italicized if that is more convenient. Finally, we include an appendix in the research report for statistical computations and other relevant material required by the instructor.

In most other respects, however, we have used APA style (for example, for references and citations). Of course, if students are writing for publication, there is no substitute for the APA publication manual. We also recommend R. J. Sternberg's *Psychologist's Companion* (Cambridge University Press), an engaging introduction to all aspects of professional writing by a psychologist who has been successful in them all. Whether one is writing a paper for a course or a journal, the classic reference is W. Strunk, Jr., and B. White's *Elements of Style* (Prentice-Hall)—a gem of a book that belongs on every author's desk. If you use WordPerfect 5.1, another resource is R. A. Smith's "Formatting APA Pages in WordPerfect 5.1" (*Teaching of Psychology*, 1992, Vol. 19, pp. 190–191).

## Acknowledgments

We thank three outstanding teachers—Anne Skleder (Alvernia College), Bruce Rind (Temple University), and Peter Crabb (Penn State University, Abington-Ogontz)—for preparing the drafts of sample papers reprinted here. We thank MaryLu Rosenthal for advising us through all four editions about the methods and means available for a literature search in a modern college library, and we thank the staff of Temple University's Paley Library and the Memorial Library of Radnor Township for their assistance. We thank Donna Shires for personal tips on using PsycLIT. We thank the following consultants whose suggestions have improved one or more editions of our book: John B. Best, Eastern Illinois University; Scott D. Churchill, University of Dallas; Nancy Eldred, San Jose State University; David

Goldstein, Duke University; John Hall, Texas Wesleyan University; James W. Kalat, North Carolina State University; Allan J. Kimmel, Fitchburg State College; Joann Montepare, Tufts University; Quentin Newhouse, Jr., Bowie State University; Arthur Nonneman, Asbury College; Edgar O'Neal, Tulane University; Rick Pollack, Merrimack College; Maureen Powers, Vanderbilt University; Robert Rosenthal, Harvard University; Gordon W. Russell, University of Lethbridge; Helen Shoemaker, California State University at Hayward; and John Sparrow, State University of New York at Geneseo. We thank Ken King of Wadsworth Press for his support of the first two editions of *Writing Papers* and James Brace-Thompson of Brooks/Cole for his support of the subsequent editions, and we thank Margaret Ritchie for her skillful editing.

We do not always specify the publication dates for reference books in our own narrative but instead advise students to seek the latest edition available and thus avoid consulting outdated material. In addition to the APA manual (which was useful in reminding us of technical points we might have forgotten to mention), we also found the following books helpful: R. Barrass, *Scientists Must Write* (Wiley, 1978); R. W. Bly and G. Blake, *Technical Writing: Structure, Standard, and Style* (McGraw-Hill, 1982); V. Dumond, *Elements of Nonsexist Usage: A Guide to Inclusive Spoken and Written English* (Prentice-Hall, 1990); B. L. Ellis, *How to Write Themes and Term Papers* (Barron's, 1989); D. E. Fear, *Technical Writing* (Random House, 1973); H. R. Fowler, *The Little, Brown Handbook* (Little, Brown, 1983); J. Gibaldi and W. S. Achtert, *MLA Handbook for Writers of Research Papers* (Modern Language Association, 1988); K. W. Houp and T. E. Pearsall, *Reporting Technical Information* (Macmillan, 1984); C. Hult and J. Harris, *A Writer's Introduction to Word Processing* (Wadsworth, 1987); S. Kaye, *Writing Under Pressure: The Quick Writing Process* (Oxford University Press, 1989); M. H. Markel, *Technical Writing: Situations and Stratetgies* (St. Martin's Press, 1984); M. McCormick, *The New York Times Guide to Reference Materials* (Dorset, 1985); D. J. D. Mulkerne and D. J. D. Mulkerne, Jr., *The Term Paper* (Anchor/Doubleday, 1983); L. A. Olsen and T. N. Huchin, *Principles of Communication for Science and Technology* (McGraw-Hill, 1957); J. G. Reed and P. M. Baxter, *Library Use: A Handbook for Psychology* (American Psychological Association, 1992); B. Spatt, *Writing from Sources* (St. Martin's Press, 1987); K. L. Turabian, *A Manual for Writers of Term Papers, Theses and Dissertations* (University of Chicago Press, 1955); and J. E. Warriner, *Handbook of English* (Harcourt, Brace, 1951).

Finally, we thank the many users of this manual. Your comments and suggestions have helped us to improve each new edition. We again invite instructors and students to send us comments and suggestions for further improvements.

*Ralph L. Rosnow*
*Mimi Rosnow*

# CHAPTER ONE

# Getting Started

Writing papers to fulfill course requirements means knowing what is expected of you and then formulating a plan to accomplish your goal on schedule. This chapter will include some simple do's and don'ts to help you avoid pitfalls and to ensure that the assignment will be completed on time and that it will represent your best work.

## Where to Begin

There was once an intriguing character named Joe Gould, who, after graduating from Harvard in 1911 and trying his hand at a number of failed endeavors, moved to New York and began to hang around Greenwich Village coffee shops. He told people that he had mastered the language of seagulls, and in fact he did an uncanny imitation of one. He was best known, however, for an ambitious project he claimed to be compiling, called the "Oral History of Our Times." He boasted of having accumulated a stack of notebooks that stood seven feet tall, and he carried brown paper bags with him that, he said, contained research notes.

Joe Gould died in a psychiatric hospital while doing his seagull imitation. Some years later, in a *New Yorker* profile by Joseph Mitchell, it was revealed that Joe Gould never started his "Oral History," his notebooks were a myth, and his brown bags merely contained other bags and yellowed newspaper clips. For students with required writing assignments, Joe Gould is a metaphor for most challenging aspect of any project, which is how to get started.

To begin your project, you need some clear objectives. Here is a checklist of questions to focus your approach:

◆ What is the purpose of the required assignment?
◆ Do I choose the theme or topic, or will it be assigned by the instructor?
◆ How long should the paper be?
◆ Will interim papers (for example, a proposal and progress reports) be required, and when are they due?

◆ When is the final report due, and how does this date mesh with my other requirements (for example, exams and other papers)?

You can talk with other students about their impressions, but the person who knows *exactly* what is expected of you is the instructor. Before you turn on a word processor or sharpen any pencils, articulate what you understand the assignment to be and ask the instructor if your understanding is accurate.

## Focusing on Your Objective

Thinking through an assignment will sharpen the intellectual process. To help you focus on your particular objective, it is well to understand the differences between the essay and the research report and the different varieties of each of these forms. If you are writing an undergraduate thesis or a master's thesis, your paper will probably contain features of *both* essays and research reports. Let us start with the general differences between the essay and the research report (see Exhibit 1), which will concentrate your efforts on whichever project you have been assigned.

One distinction highlighted in Exhibit 1 is that a literature search usually forms the core of the essay, while data form the core of the research report. The literature search for the research report typically involves a few key studies that serve as a theoretical starting point, so you can expect to spend a lot more time in the library if you are writing an essay. Of course, you still must spend time in the library if you are writing a research report, because you will need to look up background information. If you are writing an undergraduate thesis or a master's thesis, you will be expected to do a thorough search of the relevant literature. We will show how this is done in the next chapter.

A second distinction is that the composition of the essay, although somewhat formal, is more flexible than that of the research report, which has a much more standardized structure. Essays are flexible because there are different types that represent different objectives. Instructors expect the structure of the research report to conform to a general tradition that has evolved over many years. As a consequence, research reports typically include an abstract (that is, a brief summary), an introduction, a method section, a results section, a discussion of the results, and a list of the references cited.

The final distinction noted in Exhibit 1 is that the essay puts issues and ideas into the context of a particular theme or thesis, whereas the objective of the research report is to describe your empirical investigation to others. The theme in a research report usually involves testable hypotheses. What you found in your research must be put into the context of these hypotheses, but the same approach is not used as that used when writing an essay. We will have more to say about this last point later.

**EXHIBIT 1**   Differences between essays and research reports

| Essay | Research Report |
|---|---|
| 1. Based on literature search; no hard data of your own to interpret | 1. Based on data that you have collected; literature search involving only a few key studies |
| 2. Structured by you to fit your particular topic | 2. Structured following a traditional form |
| 3. Puts ideas into the context of a particular thesis | 3. Reports your own research findings to others |

# Three Types of Essays

If this were an English course, you would be taught about three types of essays, called the expository, the argumentative, and the case study. Each has its own objective. In psychology courses, however, student essays are often expected to have some characteristics of more than just one type. For example, Anne Skleder's sample paper in Appendix A (beginning on page 87) has at least a flavor of all three types, although it is primarily an expository essay.

First, the objective of an *expository essay* is to inform the reader on a specific subject or theme—in Anne's case, two views of intelligence. The word *expository* means to "expound," "set forth," or "explain." Expository essays call for accessibility in writing—like the articles that are in the science section of the *New York Times* each Tuesday, but in more detail and with full citations. Anne does not begin by writing, "I am going to explain two views of intelligence." That is, in fact, her aim (implicit in the title of her paper), but her opening paragraph shows elegance and artistry and thus draws the reader into the exposition. Other examples of expository essays might be "Basic Differences Between Operant and Classical Conditioning" and "The Role of the Teacher's Expectations in the Students' Academic Performance." Each title promises to inform the reader about some topic.

Second, the objective of persuading the reader to accept a particular point of view calls for an *argumentative essay*. In Anne's paper, there is an implicit argument for what she terms the "multiplex approach." Another example of this type of essay might be one that argued the cost-effectiveness of behavior therapy versus a more time-consuming psychotherapeutic approach. In psychology courses, argumentative essays usually attempt either to advance or to challenge the applicability of some theoretical idea in a realm beyond that for which it was originally intended. Such essays ask readers either to form a new view or to change their minds about a particular theoretical idea. If you are writing a primarily argumentative essay, be sure to express all viewpoints fairly, and not just in a "take it or leave it" fashion. Show that you recognize gray areas as you develop your position, and present documentation to support it. If you are arguing against a particular viewpoint, you can collect specific quotations to illustrate that you have represented it accurately. Otherwise, you might be accused of making a "straw man argument," which means that you represented the other side in a false, unfair, or misleading way to buttress your personal view. Before you begin to write, it is usually a good idea to argue your point of view with someone who is a good listener and promises to be very critical. Jot down questions and counterarguments while they are fresh in your mind so that you can deal with them in your paper.

Third, the purpose of the *descriptive essay* is to define (or describe) its topic. Describing (defining) the topic is a part of virtually every essay and research report, although in the descriptive essay it is the sole (or at least the primary) aim. Generally speaking, descriptive essays are frequently (but not always) shorter than expository or argumentative essays, and it is not often that a purely descriptive essay is required as a term paper. Articles in encyclopedias resemble descriptive essays. In areas of clinical psychology, you will find various combinations of descriptive and expository forms in case study reports (which are also descriptive research reports). If you are interested in reading classic examples, start with Sigmund Freud's essays, such as his case study of the "Wolf-Man," a Russian aristocrat who as a youth developed a wolf phobia and as an adult was psychoanalyzed by Freud (*The Wolf-Man and Sigmund Freud*, edited by M. Gardiner, Penguin Books, 1973).

Incidentally, creative ability is valued in science just as it is in English courses. But when explaining or describing in science, you want to be accurate and avoid flights of fancy. An effective essay in psychology is also not vague but incorporates specific examples and exact quotations to support ideas.

## Three Types of Research Reports

Researchers make fine distinctions among the various kinds of research approaches (for example, the laboratory experiment, the field experiment, the sample survey approach, the intensive case study, the archival study), and you will find examples of two such approaches in Appendixes B (a field experiment) and C (an archival study). Over and above these fine differences is another distinction among three broad types of research, called the descriptive, the relational, and the experimental. Each of these has its own objective, reflected in the research report, although the report may also contain a flavor of more than one type.

First, the purpose of the *descriptive research report* (like that of the descriptive essay) is to map out its subject. In Appendix C, Peter's report describes the content of pictorial representations of gender and work in children's books. The focus of the report is descriptive, but mapping out the relation between gender and the type of work activity implies a kind of relational flavor. Another illustration of a descriptive study would be a report of observations of freshman students thrown together for the first time as roommates in a dormitory. An education student or a psychology student specializing in child psychology might be interested in studying children's failure in school. The student could begin by spending a good deal of time observing the classroom behavior of children who were doing poorly. Careful mapping out of the behavior of failing pupils might lead to theoretical ideas about how to revise our concepts of classroom failure, to suggestions of factors that may have contributed to the development of failure, and perhaps to hypotheses for relational and experimental research concerning the remediation of failure.

The careful description of behavior is usually a necessary first step in the development of a program of research. Sooner or later, however, someone will want to know *how* what happens behaviorally is related to other variables. That is the objective of the *relational research report*, which examines how events are related or how behavior is correlated with another variable. An example might be the report of an observational study of how first-year college students have behaved differently toward one another over time; the factor of time would be one variable, and the students' behavior would be the correlated variable. In our other continuing example, the education or psychology student who was interested in failure in school might note for each pupil (a) whether the child was learning and (b) the degree to which the teacher had been exposing the child to the material to be learned. The finished report would examine the relationship between (b) and (a), that is, the amount of the pupils' exposure to the material to be learned and the amount of such material that they did in fact learn.

Thus we can say that descriptive reports tell *how things are*, while relational reports tell *how things are in relation to other things*. The purpose of the third type, the *experimental research report*, is to tell *how things get to be the way they are*. Bruce Rind's report of a field experiment in Appendix B illustrates this objective. Another example would be if you were interested in doing laboratory research with animals; you might report on how social behavior in rats is affected by manipulation of the animals' reinforcement schedules. If Peter's descriptive study (Appendix C) whets your interest, you might develop an experiment (as he implies at the end of his paper) to examine how illustrations of work episodes affect children's expectations, attitudes, and behavior.

## Scheduling Time

Once you have a clear sense of your objective, the next step is to set some deadlines so you do not end up like Joe Gould, who was so paralyzed by inertia that he accomplished nothing. In *The Shaping of a Behaviorist* (New York University Press, 1984), the celebrated psychologist B. F. Skinner recollected how he had sought to discipline himself by developing a very strict regimen when he entered Harvard University as a graduate student in 1928:

> I had done what was expected of me in high school and college but had seldom worked hard. Aware that I was far behind in a new field, I now set up a rigorous schedule and maintained it for almost two years. I would rise at six, study until breakfast, go to classes, laboratories, and libraries with no more than fifteen minutes unscheduled during the day, study until exactly nine o'clock at night and go to bed. (p. 5)

No one expects you to develop a schedule as stringent as Skinner's was when he was a student. However, once you know what is expected of you, you need to set specific deadlines that you feel you can meet. You know your own energy level and thought patterns, so play to your strengths. Are you a morning person? If so, block out some time to work on your writing early in the day. Do you function better at night? Then use the late hours of quiet to your advantage. Allow extra time for other pursuits by setting realistic dates by which you can reasonably expect to complete each major part of your assignment. Write the dates on your calendar; many students also find it useful to post the dates over their desks as daily reminders.

How do you know what tasks to schedule? If you look again at the three papers in Appendixes A, B, and C, you will infer that writing an essay calls for a quite different schedule from writing a research report. Writing an essay requires spending a lot of time in the library accumulating source materials, so you will need to leave ample time for that task. Here are some hints about what to schedule on your calendar:

Completion of proposal for essay
Completion of library work
Completion of first draft of essay
Completion of revised draft(s) of essay
Completion of final draft of essay

If you are writing a research report, set aside time for these major tasks:

Completion of proposal for research
Completion of ethics review
Completion of data collection
Completion of data analysis
Completion of first draft of research report
Completion of revised draft(s) of research report
Completion of final draft of research report

Note that both schedules of tasks allow time between the first and final drafts to distance yourself from your writing. Organizing, writing, and revising will take time. Library research does not always go smoothly; a book or a journal article you need might be unavailable. Data collection and analysis can also run into snags: the ethics review might take time, research subjects might not cooperate, or a computer you need might be down. These schedules allow you to return to your writing assignment with a fresh perspective as you polish the first draft and check for errors in logic, flow, spelling, punctuation, and grammar. By scheduling your time in this way, you should not feel pressured by imaginary deadlines—or surprised as the real deadline approaches.

If you get started early, you will also have time to track down hard-to-find reports (called the *fugitive literature* in the next chapter) or to locate an instrument you need. If you want to use a specific test protected by copyright, you will need to give yourself time to get written permission from the publisher to use the test. Instruments that require advanced training to administer or interpret are usually unavailable to undergraduate students, but there are a great many psychological measures that *are* available to students. For example, if you were doing empirical research in social or personality psychology, two relevant books might be M. E. Shaw and J. M. Wright's *Scales for the Measurement of Attitudes* (McGraw-Hill, 1967) and J. P. Robinson, P. R. Shaver, and L. S. Wrightsman's *Measures of Personality and Social Psychological Attitudes* (Academic Press, 1991). Each book contains useful paper-and-pencil measures and provides information about the validity and reliability of each measure.

For a catalog of tests and measures that you can find in journal articles and reports, see the *Directory of Unpublished Experimental Mental Measures* (American Psychological Association, Vols. 1–6, 1995–1996). Volume 6, compiled by B. A. Goldman and D. F. Mitchell, lists nearly 1,700 psychological instruments that are available for use in a wide variety of research situations, including measures of educational, psychological, social, and vocational adjustment, and measures of aptitude, attitude, concept meaning, creativity, personality, problem solving, status, and so on. Exhibit 2 shows six measures from this volume, and enough information is given to help you track down any particular instrument.

Starting early will also give you time to write to an author for follow-up articles if you think you need them. (Many students are surprised to learn that they can actually write to an author of a research study and ask about the author's most recent work.) Another word of advice: Instructors have heard all the excuses for a late or badly done paper, so do not expect much sympathy if you miss the final deadline. If you expect to ask the instructor for a letter of recommendation for graduate school or a job, you certainly do not want to create an impression of yourself as unreliable.

## Choosing a Topic

The next step is to choose a suitable topic. The selection of a topic is an integral part of learning, because usually you are free to explore experiences, observations, and ideas to help you focus on specific questions or issues that

## EXHIBIT 2 Synopses of experimental mental measures

**3678**
**Test Name:** JOB CAREER KEY
**Purpose:** To provide a test of information about a wide variety of occupations.
**Number of Items:** 157
**Format:** A multiple-choice format is used
**Reliability:** Kuder-Richardson formulas ranged from .43 to .91. Test–retest (4 months) reliability (N = 19) was .62.
**Author:** Yanico, B. J., and Hardin, S. I.
**Article:** College students' self-estimated and actual knowledge of gender traditional and nontraditional occupation: A replication and extension.
**Journal:** *Journal of Vocational Behavior*, June 1986, 28(3), 229–240.
**Related Research:** Blank, J. R. (1978). Job-career key: A test of occupational information. *Vocational Guidance Quarterly, 27*, 6–17.

**3723**
**Test Name:** MEIER BURNOUT ASSESSMENT
**Purpose:** To measure college student burnout.
**Number of Items:** 27
**Format** Employs a true-false format.
**Reliability:** Cronbach's alpha was .83.
**Validity:** Correlations with other variables ranged from -.13 to .62 (N = 360).
**Author:** McCarthy, M. E., et al.
**Article:** Psychological sense of community and student burnout.
**Journal:** *Journal of College Student Development*, May 1990, 31(3), 211–216
**Related Research:** Meier, S. T., & Schmeck, R. R. (1985). The burned-out college student: A descriptive profile. *Journal of College Student Personnel, 25*, 63–69.

**3705**
**Test Name:** COMPUTER ANXIETY SCALE
**Purpose:** To measure the perception held by students of their anxiety in different situations related to computers.
**Number of Items:** 20
**Format:** Each item is rated on a 5-point scale ranging from *not at all* to *very much.* All items are presented.
**Reliability:** Test-retest (10 weeks) reliability was .77. Coefficient alpha was .97.
**Author:** Marcoulides, G. A.
**Article:** Measuring computer anxiety: The Computer Anxiety Scale.
**Journal:** *Educational and Psychological Measurement*, Autumn 1989, 49(3), 733–739.
**Related Research:** Endler, N., & Hunt, J. (1966). Sources of behavioral variance as measured by the S-R Inventory of Anxiousness. *Psychological Bulletin, 65*, 336–339.

**3993**
**Test Name:** DATING ANXIETY SURVEY
**Purpose:** To assess dating anxiety in males and females.
**Number of Items:** 23
**Format:** Responses are made on a 7-point Likert scale, 1 (*being least anxious*) to 7 (*being extreme anxiety*). Includes three subscales: passive, active, and dating.
**Reliability:** Coefficient alphas ranged from .87 to .93 (males) and from .90 to .92 (females).
**Validity:** Correlations with other variables ranged from −.38 to .65.
**Author:** Calvert, J. D., et al.
**Article:** Psychometric evaluations of the Dating Anxiety Survey: A self-report questionnaire for the assessment of dating anxiety in males and females.
**Journal:** *Journal of Psychopathology and Behavioral Assessment*, September 1987, 9(3), 341–350.

**3710**
**Test Name:** HASSLES SCALE
**Purpose:** To identify the personal severity of daily hassles as an index of student stress.
**Number of items:** 117
**Format:** Respondents indicate on a 3-point scale the severity of each relevant daily hassle. Provides two scores: frequency and intensity.
**Reliability:** Average test-retest reliabilities were .79 (frequency) and .48 (intensity).
**Author:** Elliott, T. R., and Gramling, S. E.
**Article:** Personal assertiveness and the effects of social support among college students.
**Journal:** *Journal of Counseling Psychology*, October 1990, 37(4), 427–436.
**Related Research:** Kanner, A., et al. (1981). Comparison of two modes of stress measurement: Daily hassles and uplifts versus major life events. *Journal of Behavioral Medicine, 4*, 1–39.

**4431**
**Test Name:** PROCRASTINATION INVENTORY
**Purpose:** To measure procrastination in work-study, household chores, and interpersonal responsibilities.
**Number of Items:** 54
**Format:** Five-point self-rating scales. Sample items presented.
**Reliability:** Alpha was .91.
**Validity:** Correlations with other variables ranged from .41 (self-control) to .62 (effective study time).
**Author:** Stoham-Salomon, V., et al.
**Article:** You're changed if you do and changed if you don't: Mechanisms underlying paradoxical interventions.
**Journal:** *Journal of Consulting and Clinical Psychology*, October, 1989, 57(5), 590–598.
**Related Research:** Sroloff, B. (1963). *An empirical research of procrastination as a state/trait phenomenon.* Unpublished Master's Thesis, Tel-Aviv University, Israel.

will sustain your curiosity and interest as you work on your project. If you want to play detective, you may find prematurely abandoned ideas in research articles, such as when the researchers used statistical tests that were insensitive to the obtained effects. If you suspect this problem, you can look for clues using only a calculator and the raw ingredients in the published article. To learn more about how to do this kind of detecting, see R. L. Rosnow and R. Rosenthal's "Computing Contrasts, Effect Sizes, and Counternulls on Other People's Published Data: General Procedures for Research Consumers" (*Psychological Methods*, 1996, Vol. 1, pp. 331–340).

Ideas can also be thrust on us in unexpected ways—called *serendipity*, which is a lucky inspiration (the word comes from *Serendip*, once the name for Sri Lanka, because it was claimed that the three princes of Serendip were constantly making lucky discoveries). A book on this subject is *Serendipity: Accidental Discoveries in Science*, by R. M. Roberts (Wiley, 1989). For example, Edwin H. Land, the inventor of the Polaroid Land camera, was first inspired to think about such a camera after his 3-year-old daughter asked him why an ordinary camera could not produce pictures instantly. Another book to stimulate your creative thinking is S. W. Huck and H. M. Sandler's *Rival Hypotheses: Alternative Interpretations of Data Based Conclusions* (Harper & Row, 1979).

In considering a suitable topic, beware of a few pitfalls; the following are do's and don'ts that might make your life easier as you start choosing a topic:

◆ Use the indexes and tables of contents of standard textbooks as well as your class notes for initial leads or ideas you would like to explore more fully.
◆ Choose a topic that piques your curiosity.
◆ Make sure your topic can be covered in the available time and in the assigned number of pages.
◆ Don't be afraid to ask your instructor for suggestions.
◆ Don't choose a topic that you know other students have chosen; you will be competing with them for access to the library's source material—as well as for a good grade.

## Shaping the Topic

Choosing too broad or too narrow a topic will surely add difficulties and will also mean an unsatisfactory result. A proposed essay that is too broad—for example, "Freud's Life and Times"—would try to cover too much material within the limited framework of the assignment and the time available to complete it. A specific aspect of Freud's theoretical work would prove a more appropriately narrowed focus for treatment in an essay for a course requirement.

In narrowing the essay topic, do not limit your discussion just to facts that are already well known. There are two simple guidelines:

◆ Be sure that your topic is not so narrow that reference materials will be hard to find.
◆ Be guided by your instructor's advice because the instructor can help you avoid taking on an unwieldy topic.

If you approach instructors with several concrete ideas, you will usually find them glad to help tailor those ideas so that you, the topic, and the project format are compatible. Here are examples of how you might shape the working title of a proposed essay for a one-semester course:

### Unlimited Topic (Much Too Broad)

"Psychological Theories of Sigmund Freud"

### Slightly Limited Topic

"Freud's Theory of Dreams"

### Limited to 20-Page Paper

"Freud's Theory of Oedipal Conflict Applied to Mental Health"

### Limited to 10-Page Paper

"Freud's Theory of Infantile Sexuality"

You can always polish the title later, once you have finished your library search and have a better sense of the topic. Here is another example of shaping a topic for a one-semester course. This time the assignment is for an empirical research project:

### Unlimited Topic (Too Broad for a Term Project)

"Why Do Humans and Animals Yawn?"

### Slightly Limited Topic

"When Do Humans Yawn?"

### Adequately Limited Topic

"When Do Baboons in Zoos Yawn?"

(Incidentally, if this particular topic sounds interesting, you might begin by reading R. Baenninger's "Some Comparative Aspects of Yawning in *Betta splendens* [Siamese fighting fish], *Homo sapiens* [humans], *Panthera leo* [lions], and *Papio sphynx* [baboons]," *Journal of Comparative Psychology*, 1987, Vol.

101, pp. 349–354; and R. Baenninger, S. Binkley, and M. Baenninger's "Field Studies of Yawning and Activity in Humans," *Physiology and Behavior*, 1996, Vol. 59, pp. 421–425.)

If you are currently enrolled in a research methods course, your text probably discusses criteria for assessing the merits of hypotheses. A detailed discussion is beyond the scope of this manual, but we can mention three criteria. First, your hypotheses should be grounded in credible ideas and facts. In other words, you must do a literature search to find out whether your hypotheses are consistent with the accepted findings. Second, you need to state your hypotheses in a precise and focused way. To ensure that you are using terms correctly, you can consult resources in the library. To ensure that your hypotheses are focused, you can consult your instructor, who will show you how to use "Occam's razor" to cut away unwieldy words and ideas. Third, your hypotheses and predictions must be falsifiable if they are incorrect; hypotheses that are not refutable by any empirical means are considered unscientific, for example, "All behavior is a product of the good and evil lying within us."

## Knowing Your Audience and Topic

All professional writers know that they are writing for a particular audience. This knowledge helps them determine the tone and style of their work. Think of a journalist's report of a house fire and contrast it with a short story describing the same event. Knowing one's audience is no less important when the writer is a college student and the project is an essay or a research report. The main audience is your instructor. Should you have any questions about the instructor's grading criteria, find out what they are before you start to work.

For example, in a course on research methods (designated as a "writing course"), one instructor's syllabus contained the following grading criteria for different parts of the finished report (the numbers in parentheses are percentages):

*Abstract*
  Informativeness (5)
*Introduction*
  Clarity of purpose (10)
  Literature review (10)
*Method*
  Adequacy of design (10)
  Quality and completeness of description (10)
*Results*
  Appropriateness and correctness of analysis (10)
  Use of tables or figures (5)
  Clarity of presentation (10)

*Discussion*
    Interpretation of results (10)
    Critique/future directions (10)
*Miscellaneous*
    Organization, style, references, etc. (5)
    Appendix (5)

This kind of information enabled the students to concentrate on different parts of the assignment in the same way that the instructor would concentrate on them when evaluating the reports. This information can also serve as a checklist for you to make sure that everything of importance is covered adequately in your finished report. Not every instructor will provide such detailed information about grading, but this manual can help you compose your own refined checklist.

## Cultivating a Sense of Understanding

Let us assume that you know what your main audience—your instructor—expects of you. Now you must try to develop more than a superficial understanding of your topic. The more you read about it and discuss your ideas with friends, the more you will begin to cultivate an intuitive understanding of the topic. In the next chapter we describe how to use library resources to nurture this understanding. Here are three tips to get you started:

◆ Many writers find it helpful to keep several 3 × 5 cards handy for jotting down relevant ideas that suddenly occur to them. This is a good way to keep your subject squarely in your mind.

◆ You must also comprehend your source material, so equip yourself with a good desk dictionary, and turn to it routinely whenever you come across an unfamiliar word. It is a habit that will serve you well.

◆ While you shop for a dictionary, you might also buy a thesaurus. It can be useful as an index of terms in information retrieval (discussed in Chapter 2) as well as a treasury of synonyms and antonyms when you write.

# CHAPTER TWO

# Using the Library

Knowing about the many resources available in the library and knowing how to use them will allow you to gauge the effort it will take to accomplish your task. If you know how to use them, recent technological advances in library research can save you time and effort. This chapter considers traditional and innovative resources to help you use the library most effectively.

## Getting Oriented

You have conceived an idea for a project, have explored the idea with your instructor, and must submit a written proposal. In the next chapter we will discuss the nature of the proposal for an essay topic or a research study. However, before you begin drafting your proposal, you will need to spend some time researching your topic in the library. Later on, you will have to spend additional time in the library to gather the information needed to flesh out your final paper.

Some students become immobilized by anxiety because they are unfamiliar with library resources and how to use them. The more they think about the seemingly monumental task before them, the more anxious and disoriented they become. By analogy, there was a centipede who was out for his morning walk when he was interrupted by a grasshopper. "I've been watching you for some time," the grasshopper said, "and I wondered how you get where you are going with so many legs." The centipede thought about it, thought about it some more, and became so anxious that he could no longer walk.

The lesson is that to finish your project on schedule, you should not chew over and over the difficulty of what lies ahead but instead have a sense of where you are going and of how to take one step at a time toward that goal. If you have not set foot in your college library, now is the time to get oriented. For example, you might ask at the information desk if there is a student tour or a fact sheet (and floor plan) describing where to find things. You can also sketch your own floor plan as you begin to orient yourself.

# Plan of the Library

It is not convenient to return to the information desk every time you have a question, so you should be aware of other places you can turn for assistance. Staff members (often called *information specialists*) are also available in specialized areas of the library. For example, many libraries have a *reference desk,* and some libraries still have a *catalog desk*—although in many college and community libraries the card catalog has been replaced by an automated catalog and computers. Whatever the name of the area, each provides specialized help. Don't be afraid to ask for guidance; professional librarians derive personal satisfaction from being helpful and informative.

Here are tips to get you started as you orient yourself to the specialized areas of your library (although not all college libraries have all these areas):

◆ The *reference desk* is where you will find staff members who are true generalists and can answer all manner of questions or point you to sources that will help you answer them yourself. They may, for example, suggest general reference works that are "not circulated" (cannot be checked out) but can be used in a specified section of the library. The reference desk in some libraries is where you will find specialized indexes, for example, business periodical indexes and indexes of state and federal government publications. If you want to know about borrowing material that is unavailable in your library, this is where you ask about *interlibrary loan.*

◆ The *circulation desk* is where you check out books and other materials, return books, and take care of overdue notices. Bring an ID with you.

◆ If your library has a *catalog desk,* you will find the *card catalog* nearby; this is the name for the miles and miles of index cards that appear in alphabetical order in file drawers. In most college libraries, the card catalog has been replaced by computers that contain the automated catalog, which simply means that the same information that previously appeared on cards is accessed by a computer.

◆ The *reserve area* is for books, photocopies of journal articles, tests, and so on that your instructor has placed "on hold" (not to be circulated). You can examine this material only in the library and usually for a specified period (for example, two hours).

◆ The *current periodicals area* is where you will find recent issues of journals, magazines, and newspapers. In some libraries (called *virtual libraries*), journals and periodicals (and maybe even books) can be perused electronically, a process that conserves space and prevents the problem of missing or damaged copies. Virtual libraries share their resources through interconnected computers, so they expand the storehouse of available information.

You should also find out where *photocopiers* are located and whether you need to bring coins or purchase a card in order to use them. It is a lot easier to photocopy a page from a journal or book than to copy passages by hand.

# How Material Is Cataloged

Using the card catalog is the old-fashioned way of finding what is available in the library. The modern way is to use the automated catalog, a user-friendly, menu-driven computerized system that provides access to information by having you key in the answers to simple questions shown on the screen. Some automated catalogs are designed specifically for a given library, and some are generic designs sold by vendors. Some of these systems leave a lot to be desired, but most college and community libraries are trying to replace the card catalog with computerized systems, particularly for their current acquisitions.

Computer-readable catalogs make life easier for library staff members (who must maintain the catalog) and also for patrons. You will not have to enter a complete title, author, or subject, but type in only a word, a last name, or a phrase. The computer will then help you find what you are looking for; typically there is a "Help" key you can press if you get confused. The simplest way to find out just how easy it is to use your library's computer-readable catalog is to try it.

The card catalog, on which the computerized system is based, is a file of alphabetized 3 x 5 cards that tell you what is in the library and where to find it. Libraries that still rely on the card catalog system may have a separate catalog for their periodicals (journals, magazines, and newspapers)—that is, a *serials catalog* (possibly in a book or microfilm format of alphabetized listings) that you can request at the reference desk. Exhibits 3 and 4 show the same book (*Pygmalion in the Classroom,* a work by Robert Rosenthal and Lenore Jacobson) as it appears on the computer-readable catalog at Temple University's Paley Library and as it would appear in the card catalog.

Card catalogs contain three types of cards: (a) author cards, (b) title cards, and (c) subject cards. If your library still has a card catalog, Exhibit 3 is what you will find if you look in the card file under either "Rosenthal, Robert" or "Jacobson, Lenore" (author card) or "*Pygmalion in the Classroom*" (title card). The card shows a *call number*: a sequence of letters and numbers specified by the Library of Congress. The card also shows the name and birth date of the first author (Rosenthal, Robert, 1933–). Beneath are the title of the work and its subtitle ("teacher expectation and pupils' intellectual development"), followed by the complete list of authors in the order in which they appear on the title page of the work. Then follows the location and name of the publisher (New York, Holt, Rinehart and Winston) and the date of copyright (1968). The remainder of the card lists further technical details for librarians.

**EXHIBIT 3**   *Sample catalog card*

---

| | |
|---|---|
| LB<br>1131<br>R585 | **Rosenthal, Robert, 1933—**<br>　　Pygmalion in the classroom; teacher expectation and pupils'<br>intellectual development [by] Robert Rosenthal [and] Lenore<br>Jacobson. New York, Holt, Rinehart and Winston [1968]<br>　　xi, 240 p. illus. 23 cm<br>　　Bibliography: p. 219–229. |

　　　　　　1. Prediction of scholastic success. 2. Mental tests. I.
Jacobson, Lenore, joint author. II. Title.

LB1131.R585　　　　372.1'2'644　　　　68–19667

Library of Congress

---

In case you are interested, the information in the middle of the card shows the number of prefatory pages (xi) and the length of the book (240 p.); it also indicates that the book contains figures or other illustrations (illus.), that it stands 23 cm. high on the shelf, and that the bibliography or list of references is on pages 219–229. The section below indicates the categories under which this book should be cataloged ("Mental tests," for example). Next is the book's Library of Congress classification number again (LB1131.R585), the Dewey decimal classification number of this work (372.1'2'644), the order number of this particular set of cards (68-19667), and from whom the cards can be ordered (Library of Congress).

By comparison with Exhibit 3, we see that the automated listing in Exhibit 4 is cluttered, but it focuses on the patron's needs and not on technical details. It shows the call number and the locations in this library's stacks where the book is stored, and it indicates that the book was borrowed by someone on May 15, 1996. Also shown is a menu of choices, including exiting, asking for the full citation, and seeing other places where the book is located. Many libraries also allow patrons to print a "hard copy" (paper copy) of what is on the screen, so that they do not have to copy the information by hand. Your library's automated listing may contain information not shown in Exhibit 4 because of the particular system used, but for further guidance, you can hit the "Help" key.

# The Library Stacks

The call number indicates where permanent material is stored in the stacks (the shelves throughout the library). The stacks are coded according to categories that coincide with the numbers and letters on the index card in the

**EXHIBIT 4    Computer-readable catalog at Temple University**

```
185 PALEY         TEMPLE ONLINE CATALOG      ALL *TITLE SEARCH
  This title: Pygmalion in the classroom; teacher expe>      has 1 citation


AUTHOR: Rosenthal, Robert, 1933–
TITLE: Pygmalion in the classroom; teacher expectation and pupils' intellectual
      development [by] Robert Rosenthal [and] Lenore Jacobson.
IMPRINT: New York, Holt, Rinehart and Winston [1968]
CALL NUMBER: LB1131.R585


                        Loan
Location                Type              Status
PALEY /PLYRES           RES-8             On Reserve
  Call Number:          LB1131.R585
PALEY /STACKS           BKS-1             On Loan        05-15-96  24:00
  Call Number:          LB1131.R585


END  - to Exit the Online Catalogue       BRF  - see locations and call numbers
FUL  - see complete citation              IND  - see list of headings
CON -  see rest of locations              CAT  - begin a new search


Enter code or CON (continuation), then press CARRIAGE RETURN
~ CLS Catalog                                                      12:42
```

*Source:* Reprinted with the permission of Paley Library, Temple University, PA.

card catalog or the computer-readable catalog. For identification, the call number also appears at the bottom of the book's spine. To locate Rosenthal and Jacobson's book (Exhibits 3 and 4), we are instructed to go to the LB section of the stacks and, next, to the more specific section in numerical (1131) and then alphanumerical order (R585) where this book is shelved. If the material we want is not in the stacks, we can ask at the reference desk for help in locating it or, if the material is lost, for help in borrowing a copy through an interlibrary loan. (Even when there is a cooperative spirit, however, you may end up waiting a long time because your request has not been given a high priority by the lending library.)

Exhibit 5 shows the two systems of classification most frequently used in U.S. libraries. For psychology students, these can be puzzling systems because psychological material is classified under several different headings. The Library of Congress system divides material into 20 major groups, and abnormal psychology books, for example, can be found under BF or RC. The Dewey decimal system classifies material under 10 headings (and abnormal psychology can be found in the 157 class).

Some libraries attempt to protect their collection of books and journals by restricting access to the stacks. You submit a form that lists the material

**EXHIBIT 5   Two systems of classification**

| Library of Congress System | | Dewey Decimal System | |
|---|---|---|---|
| A | General works | 000 | General works |
| B | Philosophy and religion | 100 | Philosophy |
| C | General history | 200 | Religion |
| D | Foreign history | 300 | Social sciences |
| E-F | America | 400 | Language |
| G | Geography and anthropology | 500 | Natural sciences |
| H | Social sciences | 600 | Technology |
| J | Political science | 700 | Fine arts |
| K | Law | 800 | Literature |
| L | Education | 900 | History and geography |
| M | Music | | |
| N | Fine arts | | |
| P | Language and literature | | |
| Q | Science | | |
| R | Medicine | | |
| S | Agriculture | | |
| T | Technology | | |
| U | Military science | | |
| V | Naval science | | |
| Z | Bibliography and library science | | |

you want to use, which a staff member will then retrieve for you. However, if you are allowed to browse in the stacks, refer to Exhibit 6. It shows the cataloging of more specific areas by both systems. Browsing can lead you to a valuable but unexpected book or to a pungent quote to illustrate some idea or point.

## Using Reference Sources

Let us explore some ways you might look for material related to your project. The old-fashioned way is to do a hand search of an index, which you may have done in high school using the *Readers' Guide to Periodical Literature*. Now, you might use a compendium of abstracts (such as the *Psychological Abstracts*) or an index of citations (such as the *Social Sciences Citation Index*). The more efficient way to do a search is by means of a machine-readable database. In this case, you will be using a computer terminal to access relevant information. This is a lot easier and quicker than a hand search because the computer allows you to combine subject terms and to exclude unwanted terms in order to focus on the topic of interest.

Exhibit 7 lists relevant databases that are available on some computer systems in college libraries. PsycINFO, which is a department of the American Psychological Association, is the parent database of PsycLIT, which is used most often in psychology. It contains some references that also appear on other systems, including the automated Social Work Abstracts and Sociological Abstracts. *Psychological Abstracts* is the printed form of the PsycLIT

**EXHIBIT 6**   *Cataloging of psychological materials*

| *Library of Congress System* | | *Dewey Decimal System* | |
|---|---|---|---|
| BF | Abnormal psychology | 00- | Artificial intelligence |
| | Child psychology | 13- | Parapsychology |
| | Cognition | 15- | Abnormal psychology |
| | Comparative psychology | | Child psychology |
| | Environmental psychology | | Cognitive psychology |
| | Motivation | | Comparative psychology |
| | Parapsychology | | Environmental psychology |
| | Perception | | Industrial psychology |
| | Personality | | Motivation |
| | Physiological psychology | | Perception |
| | Psycholinguistics | | Personality |
| | Psychological statistics | | Physiological psychology |
| HF | Industrial psychology | 30- | Family |
| | Personnel management | | Psychology of women |
| HM | Social psychology | | Social psychology |
| HQ | Family | 37- | Educational psychology |
| | Psychology of women | | Special education |
| LB | Educational psychology | 40- | Psycholinguistics |
| LC | Special education | 51- | Statistics |
| Q | Artificial intelligence | 61- | Psychiatry |
| | Physiological psychology | | Psychotherapy |
| QA | Mathematical statistics | 65- | Personnel management |
| RC | Abnormal psychology | | |
| | Psychiatry | | |
| | Psychotherapy | | |
| T | Personnel management | | |

database, but there is not an exact correspondence between the two databases. As a librarian friend put it, the advantage of PsycLIT (and other computer-readable databases) is that patrons can search to their hearts' content. College libraries that have these automated systems usually have a bank of computers reserved for patrons, although you will probably have to wait your turn to use them. You might ask in your department or at the reference desk of the library whether there are computers in other locations that will allow you to communicate with the automated system through a modem.

But suppose all you need are a few key citations to provide the basis for a working hypothesis in your proposal or in the introductory section of your research report. A good place to look for key studies is the reference section or bibliography section of a current textbook or serial (such as the *Annual Review of Psychology*). You can use your library's automated catalog to sort through their repository of books and serials. Some journals specialize in literature reviews, such as the *Psychological Bulletin,* which contains an index in the last issue of every volume. However, do not simply make a citation list of articles, because your instructor will wonder if you have even read the studies cited. Read the original work.

**EXHIBIT 7** Reference databases available on computers

| Name | Coverage |
|------|----------|
| ABI/Inform | Business and personnel management, finance, consumer information, advertising |
| Books in Print | Scholarly and trade books, including titles in press and recently out-of-print books |
| Current Contents | Contents of journals in psychology, education, philosophy, political science, law, and other areas |
| Dissertation Abstracts Online | Abstracts of doctoral dissertations and theses in the United States and abroad |
| ERIC | Educational Resources Information Center, includes references from preschool to the postdoctoral level |
| MEDLINE | References in medicine, biomedicine, and related fields |
| NTIS | U.S. Government reports of government-sponsored research in engineering, agriculture, physics, biology, public policy, personnel, management, and societal behavior (for example, attitudes) |
| PsycINFO | The parent file of PsycLIT, this is the most comprehensive source of references in all areas of psychology |
| Social Scisearch | *Social Sciences Citation Index* (*SSCI*) is the parent source of titles of works and names of authors |
| Social Work Abstracts | Social work references, including substance abuse, family, and mental health literature |
| Sociological Abstracts | Sociological literature, including overlap with PsycLIT and Social Work Abstracts |

Most students who are looking for just a few key references do not find the literature search an onerous task, but some may have the feeling they are being asked to climb Mount Everest without a Sherpa guide. If this describes you, then ask your instructor for some specific leads before you exhaust yourself searching aimlessly in the library. Using reference lists in articles and books to track down relevant citations is called the *ancestry search*. The problem is that some reference lists and bibliographies may be so old that they do not include what you want. For example, the card in Exhibit 3 notes that this book contains an 11-page bibliography. But this is a classic work and so old (see the copyright date on the catalog card) that the list of references will not be of any help if you are looking for current research.

Suppose you were looking for a more general reference work, an encyclopedia of psychology. There are, in fact, many such encyclopedias, including V. S. Ramachandan's *Encyclopedia of Human Behavior* (Academic Press, 1994); R. Harré and R. Lamb's *Encyclopedic Dictionary of Psychology* (MIT Press, 1983); B. B. Wolman's *International Encyclopedia of Psychiatry, Psychology, Psychoanalysis, and Neurology* (Van Nostrand Reinhold, 1977); and R. J. Corsini's *Encyclopedia of Psychology* (Wiley, 1984). Other useful sources outside psychology are the 10-volume *Encyclopedia of Education* (Macmillan and Free Press, 1971) and the 4-volume *International Encyclopedia of Communications* (Oxford University Press, 1989). Once you find the encyclopedias in the stacks, you can browse around for other relevant references shelved nearby. If you would like a reference book *about* reference books, ask for E. P. Sheehy's *Guide to Reference Books*; it is a comprehensive, annotated listing of reference books.

If you want the best unabridged dictionary of the English language, look for the multivolume *Oxford English Dictionary* (called the *OED*). It is a fascinating resource to thumb through if you are interested in word origins. Its purpose is to give the history of all words in the English language from the year A.D. 1150 to the publication of the *OED*. There is an abridged edition in two volumes (also published by the Oxford University Press), but you need a magnifying glass to read it. Some words in the *OED* have very different meanings today from their original meanings, and it can be psychologically informative to learn about these changes in meaning.

For example, if you look up the word *gossip*, you will find that it did not always have a pejorative or sexist connotation. It began as *God sib*, for the relation a family had with someone they chose as a godparent for one of their children. In the same way that the *d* in *God's spell* was dropped to form gospel, *gossip* is the diminutive of *God sib*. By the Elizabethan age, the word *gossip* referred to an individual relationship, typically masculine, suggesting a "tippling companion." Another meaning referred to women sharing news of a birth—men were not allowed to attend births. In later years, as the sexist stereotype took hold, gossiping came to be considered the peculiar weakness of women. To call a man a gossip was to suggest a rare character defect.

A great many other useful dictionaries and reference sources are available. For example, slang dictionaries will tell you the history of words such as *hot dog* and *meathead*. They also provide information on rhyming slang, African American slang, pig Latin, and so forth. If you are interested in information about people in the news or other prominent people, you can look in *Current Biography* or *Who's Who*. If you want to know about famous Americans from the past, you can look in the *Dictionary of American Biography* or *Who Was Who in America*. The *Dictionary of National Biography* tells about men and women in British history. Librarians can point you to other works that you may find useful. Our librarian friend reminds us to emphasize that librarians are highly skilled in helping students find material. No matter how busy the librarian looks, students should not be intimidated. Do not be afraid to approach a librarian for help in finding resource material, because that is the librarian's main purpose.

### Social Sciences Citation Index

One of the reference databases listed in Exhibit 7 is Social Scisearch; it is based on the *Social Sciences Citation Index* (*SSCI*), published by the Institute for Scientific Information. The printed version of the *SSCI* is not difficult to

**EXHIBIT 8    SSCI Citations of Pygmalion in the Classroom**

| 68 Pygmalion Classroom | | | | | |
|---|---|---|---|---|---|
| Ambady N | Psychol B | 111 | 256 | 92 | R |
| Aronson JM | J Exp S Psy | 28 | 277 | 92 | |
| Berliner DC | Educ Psych | 27 | 143 | 92 | |
| Carnelle KB | J Soc Pers | 9 | 5 | 92 | |
| Deci EL | Educ Psych | 26 | 325 | 91 | |
| Ensminge ME | Sociol Educ | 65 | 95 | 92 | |
| Epstein EH | Ox Rev Educ | 18 | 201 | 92 | |
| Feingold A | Psychol B | 111 | 304 | 92 | R |
| Gaynor JLR | J Creat Beh | 26 | 108 | 92 | |
| Goldenbe C | Am Educ Res | 29 | 517 | 92 | |
| Haring KA | T Ear Child | 12 | 151 | 92 | |
| Jussim L | J Pers Soc | 62 | 402 | 92 | |
| " | " | 63 | 947 | 92 | |
| Kershaw T | J Black St | 23 | 152 | 92 | |
| Kravetz S | Res Dev Dis | 13 | 145 | 92 | |
| Mayes LC | J Am Med A | 267 | 406 | 92 | |
| McDiarmi GW | J Teach Edu | 43 | 83 | 92 | |
| McGorry PD | Aust Nz J P | 26 | 3 | 92 | R |
| Milich R | Sch Psych R | 21 | 400 | 92 | |
| Musser LM | Bas Appl PS | 12 | 441 | 91 | |
| Schwartz CA | Library Q | 62 | 123 | 92 | R |
| Semmel MI | J Spec Educ | 25 | 415 | 92 | |
| Spangenb ER | J Publ Pol | 11 | 26 | 92 | |
| Suen HK | T Ear Child | 12 | 66 | 92 | |

*Source:* Reprinted from the *Social Sciences Citation Index,*® Year 1992, Volume 3, with the permission of the Institute for Scientific Information® (ISI), © copyright 1992.

use if the computerized version is unavailable. This continuously updated database consists of three separate but related indexes to the behavioral and social science literature as far back as 1966. The printed form shows—in alphabetical order, by the last name of the first author—the year's published literature that cited the work.

For example, if you looked up Robert Rosenthal and Lenore Jacobson's *Pygmalion in the Classroom* in the 1992 *SSCI*, under Rosenthal's name, you would find the list of entries shown in Exhibit 8. Each entry gives the author of a work that refers to this book (for example, Ambady, N.), the source of the work (*Psychological Bulletin*), the volume number (111), the beginning page number (256), the year of publication (1992), and, in this case, a code letter (*R*) designating that the work was a review of the literature. Other code letters used by the *SSCI* are C for corrections; *D* for discussions (conference items); *L* for letters; *M* for meeting abstracts; *N* for technical notes; *RP* for reprint; and *W* for computer reviews (hardware, software, and database reviews).

The absence of a code letter tells us that the work is an article, report, technical paper, or the like. The fact that Ambady's work is relatively current and a review article will make the task of doing a hand search a little easier. We can now go to the periodicals section of the library and read both Ambady's article and any relevant references cited. A companion index to the *SSCI*, the *Science Citation Index* (*SCI*), also lists citations of works not usually indexed in the *SSCI*, so it might pay you to look in both indexes.

If you are wondering when to use the *SSCI* or Social Scisearch, an example would be a literature review done by Ram Aditya for his master's thesis ("The Not-So-Good Subject: Extent and Correlates of Pseudovolunteering in Research," Temple University Psychology, 1996). This student was interested in people who volunteer but then fail to show up for research participation, also called *pseudovolunteers* and *no-shows*. He first searched some standard databases, including PsycLIT, ABI/Inform, MEDLINE, ERIC, and Dissertation Abstracts Online. He then consulted the *Social Sciences Citation Index* because he thought that people who wrote about pseudovolunteering might have cited a book published in 1975 that provided a definitive discussion about the volunteer subject. He developed a list of 218 publications that had cited this book and then pared this list to only those publications that were relevant to pseudovolunteering. He had to read all the relevant articles in order to extract the basic data he needed for his review. This was a more exhaustive search than is necessary for a course paper, but it is not unusual for a good thesis.

## Printed Abstracts and Indexes

*Psychological Abstracts,* which is the printed version of the database on which PsycLIT is based, gives synopses of works in psychology and related disciplines. Exhibit 9 shows four abstracts from a volume of *Psychological Abstracts* published in 1993: (a) an article by Anastasi (in a European journal) on the history of differential psychology; (b) a book by Spiegelman on Judaism and Jungian psychology; (c) a chapter by Foster and Brizius on women's issues; and (d) a journal article by Draper on working conditions and industrial safety. Each abstract contains information about the particular work.

For instance, Anastasi's abstract begins with a code number (27890), so you can easily find the abstract again by going back to this volume and looking up this code number. The author's name is then listed; if there were more than four authors, the fourth would be followed by *et al.* ("and others"). The first author's affiliation is given next, and then the work's title is shown, followed by the journal (or other source) in which the work appeared. If the work was based on some previously published entry in *Psychological Abstracts,* that information appears next. A synopsis of the work follows; next are the number of references and the source of the

## EXHIBIT 9    Sample abstracts from *Psychological Abstracts*

**27890. Anastasi, Anne.** (Fordham U, NY) **The differential orientation in psychology.** *Zeitschrift für Differentielle und Diagnostische Psychologie*, 1992 (Sep), Vol 13(3), 133–138. — Traces the development of differential psychology from a loosely joined bundle of topics, through an integrated field of psychology, to a distinct orientation toward all psychology. The differential orientation is characterized by (1) the recognition and measurement of variability as a fundamental property of all behavior and (2) the comparative analysis of behavior under varying environmental and biological conditions, as 1 approach to understanding the nature and sources of behavior. Major orienting concepts that can be widely applied within general psychology include the multiplicity and interaction of variables involved in behavioral effects, the overlapping of distributions, the multidimensionality of individual and group differences, and the development of individuality in relation to multiple group membership. (German abstract)

**29177. Spiegelman, J. Marvin. Judaism and Jungian psychology.** University Press of America: Lanham, MD, 1993, xi, 156 pp. ISBN 0-8191-8895-6 (hardcover).
TABLE OF CONTENTS
Introduction • Part I: Harmony • Jewish psychoecumenism (Univ. of Judaism, 1989) • A Jewish psychotherapist looks at the religious function of the psyche (Association of Orthodox Jewish Scientists, UCLA, 1989) • Struggling with the image of God (Cedars-Sinai Conference on Psychology and Judaism 1986) • Judaism and Jungian psychology: A personal experience • Part II: Disharmony • The Jewish understanding of evil in the light of Jung's psychology (1988) • Part III: Harmony and disharmony together • Julia, the atheist-communist • The medium, Sophie-Sarah *[from the publicity materials]* There has been a significant amount of commentary about the Jung who was, on the one hand, thought to harbor anti-Semitic sentiment and, on the other hand, a friend and teacher of many Jews. His school of psychology has had a large Jewish following throughout the world, including Israel. J. Marvin Spiegelman uses the works of C. G. Jung to foster a dialogue between Judaism and Christianity. He demonstrates the parallels between Jung's thought and classic Kabbalistic views on the masculine and feminine aspects of Divinity and all life; "Judaism and Jungian Psychology" supplements the work of Martin Buber and Eric Fromm in

this area of Biblical research. Spiegelman includes some of his own fiction, psychomythological in theme, from "The Tree."

**29291. Foster, Susan E. & Brizius, Jack A.** (Brizius & Foster, Private Consultant). **Caring too much? American women and the nation's caregiving crisis.** [In: (PA Vol 80:29128) *Women on the front lines: Meeting the challenge of an aging America.* Allen, Jessie & Pifer, Alan (Eds.). Urban Institute Press: Washington, DC, 1993. xv. 270 pp. ISBN 0-87766-574-5 (hardcover); 0-87766-575-3 (paperback).] pp. 47–73.
*[from the chapter]*
— as America's caregivers, women hold the family together and maintain the social structure of the country ◊ the combination of increased survival rates, lower mortality at very old ages, and women's increased labor force participation means that caregiving is no longer a potentially satisfying, if, burdensome, way of life but, instead, a crisis for an expanding proportion of women in America ◊ explores the dimensions of that crisis and examines ways in which public policy might be formulated to alleviate at least part of the burden of caregiving, which is sure to increase in the near future as our population ages.

**31608. Draper, Elaine.** (U Southern California, Los Angeles) **Fetal exclusion policies and gendered construction of suitable work.** Special Issue: Environmental justice. *Social Problems*, 1993(Feb), Vol 40(1), 90–107. —Examines fetal exclusion policies (FEPs) and argues against employers' claims that scientific research supports their definition of unacceptable risk used to exclude women from jobs requiring exposure to toxic substances. Definitions of acceptable risk in FEPs are not scientific or value-neutral, but are in fact socially constructed, and therefore reflect gender stratification, corporate control, and the culturally privileged position of the fetus. This is evident in 3 of these policies' effects: (1) They exclude only certain fertile women, not all workers at risk; (2) they give priority to fetal rights, at the expense of workers' rights; and (3) corporations see them as the least costly defense against damage suits. Also examined is problematic free choice rhetoric pervading the US Supreme Court case regarding the Johnson Controls Corporation's FEP. Conceptions and power relationships that underlie fetal exclusion are also discussed.

*Source:* Reprinted with permission of the American Psychological Association, publisher of *Psychological Abstracts*, all rights reserved, and may not be reproduced without its prior permission.

abstract. The "German abstract" in parentheses tells us that the synopsis appears in a different language from that of the original work.

The abstract of Spiegelman's book shows the table of contents and contains a note indicating that the synopsis is from publicity material supplied by the publisher. It also shows the name and location of the publisher, the

**EXHIBIT 10    ERIC document abstract from RIE (Resources in Education)**

**ERIC Accession Number**—identification number sequentially assigned to documents as they are processed.

**Author(s)**

**Title**

**Institution**—organization where document originated.

**Date Published**

**Contract or Grant Number**

**Language of Document**—documents written entirely in English are not designated, although "English" is carried in their computerized records.

**Publication Type**—broad categories indicating the form or organization of the document, as contrasted to its subject matter. The category name is followed by the category code.

**ERIC Document Reproduction Service (EDRS) Availability**—"MF" means microfiche; "PC" means reproduced paper copy. When described as "Document Not Available from EDRS," alternate sources are cited above. Prices are subject to change; for latest price code schedule see section on "How to Order ERIC Documents," in the most recent issue of RIE.

**Abstractor's Initials**

**Clearinghouse Accession Number**

**Sponsoring Agency**—agency responsible for initiating, funding, and managing the research project.

**Report Number**—assigned by originator.

**Descriptive Note**—pagination first.

**Alternate source for obtaining document**

**Journal Citation**

**Descriptors**—subject terms found in the *Thesaurus of ERIC Descriptors* that characterize substantive content. Only the major terms (preceded by an asterisk) are printed in the Subject Index.

**Identifiers**—additional identifying terms not found in the *Thesaurus*. Only the major terms (preceded by an asterisk) are printed in the Subject Index.

**Informative Abstract**

---

ED 654 321                                                    CE 123 456
Butler, Kathleen                                        Smith, B. James
**Career Planning for Women.**
Central Univ., Chicago, IL.
Spons Agency — Office of Educational Research
    and Improvement (ED), Washington, DC.
Report No. — ISBN-0-3333-5568-1; OERI-91-34
Pub Date — May 92
Contract — R1900000
Note — 30p.; An abridged version of this report was
    presented at the National Conference on
    Educational Opportunities for Women (9th,
    Chicago, IL, May 14–16, 1992).
Available from — Campus Bookstore, 123 College
    Avenue, Chicago, IL 60690 ($5.95).
Language — English, Spanish
Journal Cit — Women Today; v13 n3 p1-14 Jan 1992
Pub Type — Reports—Descriptive
(141)—Tests/Questionnaires (160)
**EDRS Price—MF01/PC02 Plus Postage.**
Descriptors — Career Guidance, *Career Planning,
    *Demand Occupations, *Employed Women,
    *Employment Opportunities, Females, Labor
    Force, Labor Market, Postsecondary Education
Identifiers — Consortium of States, *National
    Occupational Competency Testing Institute
    Women's opportunities for employment will be
directly related to their level of skill and experience
and also to the labor market demands through the
remainder of the decade. The number of workers
needed for all major occupational categories is
expected to increase by about one-fifth between 1990
and 1999, but the growth rate will vary by occupational group. Professional and technical workers are
expected to have the highest predicted rate (39 percent), followed by service workers (35 percent), clerical workers (26 percent), sales workers (24 percent),
craft workers and supervisors (20 percent), managers
and administrators (15 percent), and operatives (11
percent). This publication contains a brief discussion
and employment information (in English and in
Spanish) concerning occupations for professional and
technical workers, managers and administrators,
skilled trades, sales workers, clerical workers, and
service workers. In order for women to take advantage of increased labor market demands, employer
attitudes toward working women need to change and
women must: (1) receive better career planning and
counseling, (2) change their career aspirations, and (3)
fully utilize the sources of legal protection and assistance that are available to them.
(Contains 45 references.)
(SB)

---

**EXHIBIT 11  ERIC journal article from CIJE (Current Index to Journals in Education)**

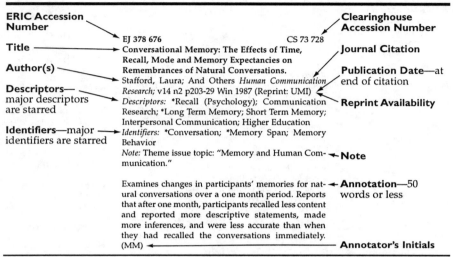

ERIC Accession Number

Clearinghouse Accession Number

EJ 378 676                                    CS 73 728

Title — Conversational Memory: The Effects of Time, Recall, Mode and Memory Expectancies on Remembrances of Natural Conversations.

Journal Citation

Author(s)

Stafford, Laura; And Others *Human Communication Research;* v14 n2 p203-29 Win 1987 (Reprint: UMI)

Publication Date—at end of citation

Descriptors— major descriptors are starred

*Descriptors:* *Recall (Psychology); Communication Research; *Long Term Memory; Short Term Memory; Interpersonal Communication; Higher Education

Reprint Availability

Identifiers—major identifiers are starred

*Identifiers:* *Conversation; *Memory Span; Memory Behavior

*Note:* Theme issue topic: "Memory and Human Communication."

Note

Examines changes in participants' memories for natural conversations over a one month period. Reports that after one month, participants recalled less content and reported more descriptive statements, made more inferences, and were less accurate than when they had recalled the conversations immediately. (MM)

Annotation—50 words or less

Annotator's Initials

*Source:* From *ERIC Resources in Education, 28,* No. 6, June 1993, copyright © 1993 Educational Resources Information Center (ERIC), U.S. Department of Education. Reprinted with permission.

copyright date, the number of prefatory pages, the length of the book, and a unique code assigned by the publisher that identifies this edition of the book (the ISBN, or International Standard Book Number). The abstract of the chapter by Foster and Brizius contains parenthetical information about the book in which it appeared and notes that the book was previously indexed in *Psychological Abstracts.* An open diamond (◊) is used to separate a quoted phrase.

If you were doing an exhaustive search on an educational topic, another useful resource would be ERIC (Educational Resources Information Center), an abstract service funded by the U.S. Department of Education. Exhibit 10 shows an annotated ERIC abstract as found in *Resources in Education* (RIE). Exhibit 11 shows an annotated ERIC abstract of a journal article; these abstracts can be found in *Current Index to Journals in Education* (CIJE).

There are print abstracts and indexes (some also automated, see again Exhibit 7) for just about every discipline and area of interest (for example, *Biological Abstracts, Art Index, Abridged Index Medicus,* and *Humanities Index*), and a librarian will be glad to direct you to the relevant indexes and abstracts. You will find useful tips on using reference databases in J. G. Reed and P. M. Baxter's chapter, "Using Reference Databases," in H. Cooper and L. V. Hedges's *Handbook of Research Synthesis* (Russell Sage, 1994, pp. 57–70). If you would like to have a comprehensive list of relevant indexes and abstracts, see M. C. Rosenthal's "Bibliographical Retrieval for the Social and Behavioral Scientist" (*Research in Higher Education*, 1985, Vol. 22, pp. 315–333). One of M. C. Rosenthal's suggestions is to make a checklist of sources already searched, so that you do not backtrack without realizing it; list the abstract or index, the years searched, and the search terms (called *descriptors*) that you used.

## Using PsycLIT

A computer search is faster and more fun than a hand search, and using a machine is really the only way to begin an exhaustive search on a given topic. If you are using PsycLIT, you might ask a librarian whether you can obtain a copy of the *PsycLIT Quick Reference Guide*; it defines symbols and commands and will lead you step-by-step through some search techniques. However, you will find that the basic system is user-friendly, and to get started, all you really need is a question that you want to answer. For example, suppose you wanted to know "What research has been done on rumor and gossip?" You can use these key words (*rumor* and *gossip*) to get you started, and looking in PsycLIT's thesaurus can save you time by focusing your search on related descriptors that are indexed in the system. This thesaurus is available in both an automated and a book form (*Thesaurus of Psychological Index Terms*, published by the American Psychological Association).

To use PsycLIT, you press keys and type things to tell the system what you want it to find. There is a tutorial that you can "boot" (start up) by pressing the "Ctrl" key and the "t" key simultaneously. You can get HELP by pressing the "F1" key; if you press the "Ctrl" and "F1" keys together, you will be shown a list of HELP topics. Pressing the "F10" key places a command menu at the bottom of the screen, which you then use directly or else press the F-key equivalents that are shown. If you press "F3" and then the highlighted letter, you will get searching information. Pressing "F7" restarts the system. Once you are into PsycLIT, the "F9" key brings up the thesaurus prompt; by entering a term, you elicit synonyms or related descriptors. The trick is to choose the appropriate descriptors and to enter them in the sequence that PsycLIT understands. You can make up your own template to keep track of the F keys and their functions, but as you work with PsycLIT, you will quickly get the hang of it.

Suppose you wanted to look up an author's name or a journal. In this case, you press "F5" and then enter the name. For example, if you wanted to look up the work of the developmental psychologist Laurence Steinberg, you would press "F5" and then type "Steinberg-Laurence" (type the hyphen but not the quotes). To type the name of a journal, you again use hyphens, for example, "Personality-and-Social-Psychology-Bulletin" (do not type the quotes). There is a "Find" prompt you get by pressing the "F2" key. Suppose you were doing experimental research in child psychology and your library subscribed to one journal in this area, the *Journal of Experimental Child*

**EXHIBIT 12    Sample abstracts downloaded from PsycLIT**

---

TI: The influence of personal characteristics on rumor knowledge and transmission among the deaf.
AU: Anthony, -Susan
IN: Gallaudet U, Washington, DC, US
JN: American-Annals-of-the-Deaf; 1992 Mar Vol 137(1) 44-47
AB: Examined among 80 deaf college students the personal characteristics on which rumor knowledge and transmission (RKT) depend in a deaf population. The author also examined whether the well-documented variable that influences RKT among hearing people, namely anxiety level, also operates among deaf people and whether additional variables specific to the culture would influence RKT. These variables were identified as type of school attended (residential or mainstream) and preferred mode of communication. Results support previous studies (e.g., M. E. Jaeger et al; see PA, Vol 66:5716) with hearing Ss on the importance of trait anxiety or generalized anxiety on RKT of specific topics. General rumor knowledge was influenced by anxiety as well as by culturally specific variables. Individual differences in overall rumor knowledge were influenced by trait or general anxiety level. (PsycLIT Database Copyright 1992 American Psychological Assn, all rights reserved)
AN: 79-32041

---

TI: Campus in crisis: Coping with fear and panic related to serial murders.
AU: Archer,-James
IN: U Florida, University Counseling Ctr, Gainesville, US
JN: Journal-of-Counseling-and-Development; 1992 Sep-Oct Vol 71(1) 96-100
AB: Describes the university and community response to the serial murders of 5 students at the University of Florida in 1990. The campus crisis management efforts, early crisis intervention activities, rumor control, the role of the media, and the long-range effects of the crisis are discussed. (PsycLIT Database Copyright 1993 American Psychological Assn, all rights reserved)
AN: 80-03592

---

*Source:* Reprinted with permission of the American Psychological Association, publisher of *Psychological Abstracts* and PsycLIT (Copyright 1967–1996 by the American Psychological Association), and may not be reproduced without its prior permission.

*Psychology.* To search this journal for your descriptor, you press "F2" and then type the key term and "Journal-of-Experimental-Child-Psychology" after the "Find" prompt. You can also use abbreviations in your search: AU = author(s); DE = descriptors; JN = journal name; PO = population.

Exhibit 12 shows two sample abstracts that were obtained by using *rumor* as the descriptor. We can use an asterisk to ask PsycLIT to get any variation of a word root or phrase (*rumor\** will retrieve *rumormonger* and *rumormongering*), and we can use a question mark (?) as a wild card symbol (*rumor?*). Used at the end of a word, the question mark allows us to retrieve a plural version of the word (for example, *rumors*); used in the middle of the word (*rumo?r*), the question mark allows us to retrieve both American (rumor) and British spellings (*rumour*). Used at both the middle and the end (*rumo?r?*), the question mark allows us to find American and British singular and plural versions. Note in the abstracts in Exhibit 12 that one abstract contains the descriptor as part of its title and synopsis, while the other abstract has the descriptor only in the synopsis. Note also that the information retrieved is similar to that in Exhibit 9. We are given the title (*TI*), the authors (*AU*), the primary author's institution (*IN*), the synopsis of the work (*AB* for "abstract"), and a code number showing the volume and entry number of the particular work in *Psychological Abstracts*.

Letting our fingers do the walking can save time and energy if we ask the right questions. For example, Donna Shires once described her experience using PsycLIT when she was a graduate student:

> I was writing a paper about how questionnaire results may be biased by the way the questions themselves are worded. Specifically, I was interested in the problem of people answering "yes" to questions that they might not really agree with. My understanding was that this problem was called *yea-saying*. Armed with this limited knowledge, I got on PsycLIT and entered the descriptor *yea-saying*. I found only two articles that addressed this topic. Because my paper required a literature review, I became a little worried. Two articles could hardly be considered a literature review. At this point, I decided to go back to some textbooks that had information on questionnaire design. Upon reading more information, I discovered that *yea-saying* was not the most general or common term for the problem I was interested in. Rather, *acquiescent response bias,* or some variation thereof, was the term of choice. When I got back on PsycLIT and plugged in *acquiescent,* I found a whole list of articles. My literature review could proceed!

Donna ran into the opposite problem in another situation, when she turned up many articles that were not relevant to what she wanted:

> I was interested in finding studies that had looked at people's attitudes toward the mentally ill. I used the descriptors *attitude\*, mentally,* and *ill* in this search. When I combined these (by first combining *mentally* and *ill* and then adding *attitude\**), PsycLIT informed me that more than 70 articles contained these terms. In looking these articles over, I found that some had to do with attitudes *of* mentally ill people, not attitudes *about* mentally ill people. When I used the descriptors *mental* and *illness* with *attitude\**, I located articles that dealt with attitudes *about* the mentally ill.

Donna learned some tricks that she has passed on to us:

◆ One way to speed up the search process is to search for only one descriptor at a time. Suppose you wanted to retrieve work on "racial prejudice." The fastest way to do this search is first to type *racial* at the "Find" prompt. Once this search is complete, type *prejudice*. Following this search, you then tell PsycLIT to find "#1 and #2" (or whatever the assigned numbers are). This approach works more efficiently than typing in *racial prejudice* as one descriptor. Also, separating your search into specific words can save you time later on. For example, let's say that you think that racial prejudice may be related to stereotyping. You do a search on *stereotype,* which is assigned the number 5. You can then tell PsycLIT to find "#1 and #5" to see what works are available on racial stereotypes.

◆ Another hint has to do with using the asterisk insert (called the *unlimited truncation symbol*). Donna also wanted to find literature on *acquiescent response bias.* Some authors used this term, but others had used acquiescence. Rather than run several searches, Donna typed *acquiescen\** at the "Find" prompt. In this way, she told PsycLIT to search for that descriptor and allowed for several different endings to the term. Therefore, articles using both *acquiescent* and *acquiescence* came up in the search.

◆ The number of articles can be a signal that your search is too narrow or too broad. If you retrieve no articles, you may be using the wrong descriptor. If you retrieve only one or two articles, you may be searching for something too specific or using the wrong descriptor. If you turn up large numbers of articles, you probably need to narrow your search. For example, if you are interested in the treatment of depression, you can specify particular types of treatment to get the number of articles down to a reasonable size.

Donna also has some good advice when it is time to download, print, or both:

◆ You will find it useful to have the complete abstract of the article as well as the citation (see again Exhibit 12). The default in PsycLIT is "citation only," which then prints the titles of all articles located in the search. You will need to change "CITN" to "ALL" to get the full abstract.

◆ To get only specific articles, enter the code number assigned to these articles by PsycLIT.

◆ If you are printing directly from the PsycLIT database to a printer, it is generally better to look over the articles and print only those that are relevant. This gives you more time to conduct searches, because most printers in libraries are not very fast.

◆ If you have your own personal computer with a floppy drive, you may be able to download information from PsycLIT and look it over at your convenience, so you can deal with large numbers of articles. This saves the most time. However, make sure that you get the full abstract when you download, because just the citation tells you little.

## The Fugitive Literature

Work that is unpublished or simply hard to find is termed the *fugitive literature* (or *gray literature*). For a thorough discussion of this subject, see M. C. Rosenthal's chapter, "The Fugitive Literature," in H. Cooper and L. V.

Hedges's *Handbook of Research Synthesis* (Russell Sage, 1994, pp. 85–94). For example, private institutions and government agencies support research that may be circulated only in technical reports. Other examples of the fugitive literature include papers that researchers present at professional meetings, as well as dissertations and theses that graduate students write. If the work you are seeking is in the interlibrary loan network, you can request that your library borrow it, but be prepared for a long waiting period.

Fugitive literature can often be tracked down, if you have the time to spare. For example, if you are familiar with an author's previous work, you can write to that person for follow-up studies, talks, technical reports, and so on. You will increase the likelihood of obtaining a response if your request is precise and convincing. Researchers receive many requests for reprints, preprints, and other information, so do not expect a busy researcher to answer a long line of questions or to send you material that is readily available in any college library.

If you are in a department that has many active researchers on the staff, it is possible that one of them is working on the very problem in which you are interested. If so, set up an appointment to discuss your interests, but be sure to do your homework on the subject first. List for yourself the questions you want to ask, and then take notes during the interview. You may be able to make a connection through the Internet with someone who knows something, but simply surfing the Net can be a real time waster. To learn how to use the Internet more efficiently to track down relevant material, see D. Kelley-Milburn and M. A. Milburn's article "Cyberspace: Resources for Psychologists on the Internet," which appeared in *Psychological Science* (1995, Vol. 6, pp. 203–211).

## Taking Notes in the Library

We have discussed locating material but not taking notes in the library. If you have the funds, the best way to ensure that your notes will be exact is to photocopy the original material. But be sure to record in a conspicuous place on the photocopy the complete citation of all you copied. You will still need to interpret what you copied, and it is often easier to make notes of your interpretation at the time you have the material in hand. Having such notes will enable you to write an accurate paper as well as one that is efficiently organized.

Making detailed notes will also help you avoid committing *plagiarism* accidentally. We will have more to say about this subject in Chapter 6, but you plagiarize intentionally when you knowingly copy or summarize someone's work without acknowledging that source. You plagiarize accidentally when you copy someone's work but forget to credit it or put it in quotation marks. Plagiarism is illegal, and you should guard against it by keeping accurate notes and giving full credit to others when it is due.

If you are taking handwritten notes in the library, use a separate index card for each quotable idea that you find as you uncover relevant material in your literature search. Many writers prefer making notes on 5 × 8 index cards because they can usually get all the information they want on the front of a large card, so it is easier to find what they want later. Exhibit 13 shows two examples of notes taken for a term paper; the student found two sections in one source for use in the paper. This exhibit will also be helpful even if you are taking notes using a laptop computer, because you still need to record background information for citations and references.

Observe that the cards are numbered "1 of 2" and "2 of 2" in the upper-right corner, and the book's call number is included at the lower left. If you have made an outline for an essay (as described in Chapter 4), you might code each card (at the lower right) with the particular section of the outline that the material on the card will illustrate (or you may color-code your cards). In this way, you can maintain a general order in your notes and avoid facing a huge stack of miscellaneous bits and pieces of information that will loom large as you try to sort and integrate the information you find in the library into a useful form. Be consistent with all the reference numbers you use; a haphazard arrangement will only slow you down when it is time to write the first draft.

The two index cards in Exhibit 13 contain a wealth of material. At the top of both cards is a complete citation. Such a citation will be required in your reference section (where you will list all the sources you have cited) and will be condensed in the citations in the paper's narrative. The top card summarizes, in the notetaker's own words, the major details of the study reported by Rosenthal and Jacobson. This synopsis ends with a quotation chosen to illustrate Rosenthal and Jacobson's conclusions. Note that the page number of the quote is included; the page number must be cited if the student decides to use this quote. On the bottom card, the student has focused the material taken from this book by asking a particular question. The lengthy quotation copied from Rosenthal and Jacobson specifically addresses the question. Notice that four dots (a period plus ellipsis points) interrupt the text halfway through the quote; they indicate that a portion of the quote has been purposely omitted by the student.

The most fundamental rule is to be thorough and systematic so that you do not waste time and energy having to return to the same book or article. Because memory is porous, it is better to photocopy or record too much than to rely on recall to fill in the gaps. Be sure your notes will make sense to you when you examine them later.

## Additional Tips

Here are some more tips to help you get started on the literature search and do it efficiently:

◆ Try to be realistic in assessing how many books and articles you will need in your literature review. Too few may result in a weak foundation for your project, but too much material and intemperate

**EXHIBIT 13    Sample note cards**

Rosenthal, Robert, and Jacobson, Lenore (1968). Pygmalion in the classroom:
Teacher expectation and pupils' intellectual development. New York: Holt,
Rinehart and Winston

*1 of 2*

Teachers at "Oak School" (an elementary school in California) were led to believe
that about 20% of students were potential "bloomers" based on their performance
on a test to pick out intellectual bloomers (or spurters). Actually, the names of the
20% had been chosen at random and the test was a nonverbal IQ test (TOGA). All
students were retested with TOGA after one semester, after a full academic year,
and after two academic years. The IQ gains of the 20% (the experimental group)
consistently surpassed the IQ gains of the remaining (control group) students.
This result is consistent with Rosenthal's self-fulfilling prophecy hypothesis
(see also Merton, R.). The authors conclude that "... one person's expectation
for another person's behavior can quite unwittingly become a more
accurate prediction simply for its having been made." (page vii)
LB1131.R585

---

Rosenthal, Robert, and Jacobson, Lenore (1968). Pygmalion in the classroom:
Teacher expectation and pupils' intellectual development. New York: Holt,
Rinehart and Winston.

*2 of 2*

What practical implications do these authors draw from their research
findings? "As teacher-training institutions begin to teach the possibility
that teachers' expectations of their pupils' performance may serve as self-
fulfilling prophecies, there may be a new expectancy created. The new
expectancy may be that children can learn more than had been believed
possible, an expectation held by many educational theorists, though for
quite different reasons .... The new expectancy, at the very least, will
make it more difficult when they encounter the educationally disadvantaged
for teachers to think, 'Well, after all, what can you expect?' The man on the
street may be permitted his opinions and prophecies of the unkempt
children loitering in a dreary schoolyard. The teacher in the schoolroom
may need to learn that those same prophecies within her may be fulfilled;
she is no casual passer-by. Perhaps Pygmalion in the classroom
is more her role." (pp. 181-182)
LB1131.R585

expectations may overwhelm you and your subject. You are writing not a doctoral dissertation or an article for publication in a journal but a required paper that must be completed within a limited time frame.

◆ How can you find out what is a happy medium between too little and too much? Talk with your instructor before you start an intensive literature search. Ask whether your plan seems realistic.

◆ Before you start your literature search, ask the instructor to recommend any key works that you should read or consult. Even if you feel confident about your topic already, asking the instructor for specific leads can prevent you from going off on a tangent.

◆ Do not expect to finish your literature search in one sitting. Students with unrealistic expectations make themselves overly anxious and rush a task that should be done patiently and methodically to achieve the best result.

◆ In planning your schedule, give yourself ample time to do a thorough job. Patience will pay off by making you feel more confident that you understand your topic well.

◆ Suppose you cannot locate the original work that you are looking for in the stacks. Some students return repeatedly to the library, day after day, seeking a book or journal article before discovering that it has been lost or stolen or is being rebound. Ask an information librarian to find the elusive material. If the original work you need is unavailable, the librarian may consult another college library. However, the material could take so long to arrive that you might miss the deadline set by your instructor (which is not an acceptable excuse).

◆ If you are looking for a specialized work, you probably will not find it in a small public library, so do not waste your time. When students spend a lot of time off-campus in public libraries and bookstores looking for source material, they usually come back with references from general texts or current mass-market books and periodicals.

◆ Follow M. C. Rosenthal's advice and keep a running checklist of sources searched, including the name of the database, the years you searched, and the search terms you used so that you don't accidentally retrace your steps.

## Library Etiquette

Before we turn to the basics of developing your proposal for an essay or a research project, here is some final advice about using the library. The golden rule of library etiquette is to respect your library and remember that others have to use it after you, which means:

◆ Never tear out pages of journals or books.
◆ Never write in library journals or books.
◆ Do not monopolize material or machines.
◆ Return books and periodicals as soon as you finish with them.

# CHAPTER THREE

# Drafting the Proposal

Once you have chosen your topic and begun your library work, the next step is to develop a proposal of what you plan to do. Some instructors feel that a brief oral presentation of your plan is sufficient. Others require a written proposal as a way of ensuring that both the instructor and you have a common understanding of your topic and procedures.

## Purpose of the Proposal

The purpose of your proposal is to tell the instructor what you would like to study and to write about in your essay or research report. However, it is not simply a one-way agreement, but an opportunity for the instructor to provide feedback and to raise questions. If you are required to do an empirical study, the proposal is also an opportunity to address ethical issues before you are permitted to collect any data. The proposal thus serves as a kind of "letter of agreement," in which you and the instructor agree that the planned project is ethically sound and methodologically feasible.

Instructors may require preliminary submissions in addition to a final proposal. They may also ask for details in addition to those illustrated in the sample proposals in this chapter. You may be asked to tell how you arrived at your ideas and why you believe the topic you selected is interesting and important. The purpose of such questions is (a) to help you crystallize your ideas, (b) to encourage you to focus on a topic you find intrinsically interesting, and (c) to make sure that these are *your* ideas.

We will have more to say about the third point in a later chapter, but it is essential that the work be your own even if it builds on, or is a replication of, previous work by others. Replications are very important in science, and they are often the basis of undergraduate theses or master's theses. However, the student is usually expected to add some personal creative touch in the form of a new hypothesis or some innovative aspect of the design.

**EXHIBIT 14** *Sample proposal for an essay*

---

Essay Proposal for (Course No.)

Submitted by Anne A. Skleder

(Date Submitted)

<u>Working Title</u>

A Comparison of Two Views of Intelligence: With Emphasis
on Gardner's Theory of Multiple Intelligences

<u>Objective</u>

My essay will compare the classic view of intelligence
with a more current view. The classic view is that there
is a common core in all measures of intelligence (called
g); theories that are consistent with this g-centric position have been dominant in psychology for many years. In
contrast to the classic approach is what I will call the
<u>multiplex view</u>, which is the position that many kinds of
intelligences are housed within the same culture (like
movies in a multiplex theater).

I will focus my discussion on one prominent example of
the multiplex view, the theory of "multiple intelligences"
developed by Howard Gardner. I will explain the nature of
his theory and also discuss criticisms of it. I will try
to give a flavor of the future direction of work in the
area of intelligence.

<u>Literature Search Strategy</u>

To locate material for this paper, I will conduct a
search using PsycLIT and ERIC and will also identify some
key papers and run an ancestry search using the automated
<u>Social Sciences Citation Index.</u> One very useful paper was
recently published in the <u>American Psychologist</u> (1996); it
contains the report of a Task Force of the American Psychological Association (headed by U. Neisser), which discusses "knowns" and "unknowns" in the nature of
intelligence.

---

# The Essay Proposal

Exhibit 14 shows the basic structure of the proposal for an essay. The working title (which can be changed later) gives an overall preview of the topic
you selected. You then discuss in more detail (although briefly) the objective

of your essay; you need to explain very clearly where you are heading and why you decided to go in that direction. And finally, the last section tells the instructor how you plan to do the literature search to familiarize yourself with the work that has already been done on your chosen topic. The instructor's comments on your proposal will continue the process of shepherding you toward your final goal.

## The Research Proposal

Exhibits 15 and 16 show the basic structure of the proposal for a research project. Although the aims of the two proposals are very different, the basic structure is similar. Each proposal starts with a working title that gives a preview of the study. The student then discusses in detail the objective of the study and leads into the hypotheses. The proposed method comes next, and any instruments to be used would be described here. If you have developed a measure, it belongs here or in an accompanying appendix. Next described is the overall plan for analyzing the quantitative or qualitative data. Finally, the student defends the ethics of the proposed research.

## Ethical Considerations

Ethical accountability is an important issue in psychology, particularly when conducting and reporting empirical research. Thus your instructor may require that you answer very specific questions in your proposal regarding the ethical conduct of the research. Broadly speaking, psychological researchers are expected to protect the dignity, privacy, and safety of their research participants and to do research that is technically sound and potentially beneficial to society. There are several excellent books on this subject, such as A. J. Kimmel's *Ethical Issues in Behavioral Research: A Survey* (Blackwell, 1996).

Here are some questions to guide you as you think about what to write in your proposal:

♦ What will the subjects be asked to do?
♦ Are there any psychological or physical risks to the subjects?
♦ Will any deception be used, and if so, why is it necessary?
♦ How will the subjects be debriefed (and "dehoaxed" if deception is used)?
♦ Will the subjects be recruited in a noncoercive way?
♦ How will the subjects be told what the purpose of the study is and that they are free to quit at any time without penalty?
♦ How will the subjects' informed consent be secured?
♦ What steps will be taken to ensure the confidentiality of the data?

## EXHIBIT 15 *Sample proposal for experimental study*

Research Proposal for (Course No.)

Submitted by Bruce Rind

(Date Submitted)

Working Title

An Experimental Study of the Effects of a Small Gift on
Tipping Responses

Objective

A recent article by Lynn in the Cornell Hotel and
Restaurant Administration Quarterly noted various techniques that servers can use to improve their tipping percentages. Most of these techniques seem to involve
boosting the customers' impressions of the server's
friendliness (e.g., a friendly touch or drawing a smiling
face on the check). I would like to experiment with
another technique in this vein, which is to present the
customer with a small gift (a fancy mint). I am also
interested in whether reciprocity is a factor moderating
the effectiveness of this technique. Reciprocity is the
idea that people feel obligated to return a favor
received, and this can be manipulated by attributing the
small gift either to the restaurant or to the generosity
of the server.

Specifically, then, I would like to test the following
two hypotheses:

1. The server's presentation of a small gift along with
the check will elicit a larger tip than if no gift is
given.

2. The attribution of such a gift to the generosity of
the server will elicit a larger tip than if the gift is
attributed to the restaurant.

Proposed Method

I have described my proposed study to the servers and
the owner of a restaurant-diner and have got their
approval. I will use a randomized design with three
groups: a no-mint control condition and two mint conditions. I will write the condition on a card, then shuffle
all the cards, and have the server draw one out of a bag

Rind   2

at the time the check is to be presented. There will 25
cards for each of the three conditions ($\underline{N}$ = 75).

One set of cards will state "no mint," which means that
the server is to present the check without a mint. A second set of cards will state "mints from me," which means
that the server is to present the mints to each member of
the dining party and say, "Here are some mints from me."
The third set of cards will have "mints from restaurant,"
which means the server is to present mints to each member
of the dining party and state, "Here are some mints from
the restaurant." The server's interaction with the customers will be limited to the presentation of the check
and the prescribed treatment.

Proposed Data Analysis

When the dining parties leave, the server will record
on the same index card used to determine the experimental
condition the amount of the bill before taxes, the tip
amount, and the number of customers at the table. The
dependent variable will be the tip percentage, which I
will calculate by dividing the amount of the tip by the
size of the check before taxes and multiplying by 100. I
will test the hypotheses using this dependent variable and
$\underline{t}$-test comparisons as implied by each hypothesis. All tips
will be the property of the servers, who have agreed to
share them equitably.

Ethical Considerations

The study involves a mild deception in that the customers are unaware of their participation in an experiment,
but I do not propose to debrief them because no potential
risk is involved. I cannot ask the people who are dining
whether they would agree to "participate in an experiment"
because that would destroy the credibility of the manipulation and render the study meaningless. The servers and the
owner will be given full details of the results.

**EXHIBIT 16** *Sample proposal for archival study*

Research Proposal for (Course No.)

Submitted by Peter B. Crabb

(Date Submitted)

Working Title

The Nature of Representations of Work and Gender in
Children's Books

Objective

Gender is an important factor determining the division
of labor in industrialized societies. I am interested in
how high-profile books for children portray work and gender, because I suspect that these portraits may reinforce
gender stereotypes. I propose to do a content analysis of
a random sample of pictures depicting both work and gender
in children's books that have received the Newbery or
Caldecott Award. I will test two hypotheses:

1. In comparison with male characters, female characters are more likely to be shown doing household work.

2. In comparison with female characters, male characters are more likely to be shown doing production work
outside the home.

Proposed Method

I will begin by photocopying illustrations that clearly
show both work and gender. Under the instructor's direction, I will create a representative sample of these
illustrations. Two students have agreed to code the illustrations for (1) the tool shown in the picture, (2) the
type of work represented (i.e., household, production, or
other), and (3) whether the person doing the work is male,
female, or unidentifiable by gender. The coders will be

Crabb 2

told that <u>household work</u> is defined as "the use of tools
in and around the home to prepare food, to clean, and to
care for family members"; <u>production work</u> as "the use of
tools outside the home for construction, agriculture, and
transportation"; and <u>other work</u> as "work that does not
qualify as either household or production, including the
use of tools for leisure activities and for protection
from the elements."

<u>Proposed Data Analysis</u>

To quantify the interrater reliability of coders, I
will use Cohen's kappa. The main results will be graphed,
and to test the hypotheses, I will use a procedure that
compares proportions.

<u>Ethical Considerations</u>

I believe there are no ethical problems because the
data are nonsensitive and in the public domain. I will
give the coders a copy of my final report, and I will com-
pensate each coder with a music tape or CD of that person's choice.

# Tempus Fugit

Because time flies when you are writing a required paper for a course, here are two final tips:

◆ Turn in your proposal on time. Instructors are also very busy people, and they (like you) schedule their work. Turning in a proposal late is like waving a red flag that signals the wrong message to your instructor. Instead of communicating that you are responsible and reliable and think clearly, this "red flag" signals that you may be none of the above.

◆ Be precise. In Lewis Carroll's *Through the Looking Glass,* Alice (of *Alice in Wonderland*) comes upon Humpty Dumpty, who uses a word in a way that Alice says she does not understand. He smiles contemptuously and says, "Of course you don't—till I tell you. . . . When *I* use a word, it means just what I choose it to mean—neither more nor less." Unlike Humpty Dumpty, you do not have the luxury of telling your instructor to "take it or leave it." Nor do you have the extra time to spare to keep resubmitting the proposal because you did not make an effort to be precise.

# CHAPTER FOUR

# Organizing the Essay

Once you have completed your library research, you are
ready to prepare a detailed outline. The imposition of form
will help you collect and refine your thoughts as you shape
the final essay. Even if you did not outline before the fact, you
can do so afterward. (If you are writing a research report, you
can skip this chapter and go on to Chapter 5.)

## Where to Start

Instructors are usually very sensitive to a weak structure or a lack of structure in essays because this flaw is so apparent in many they have read.
When an essay has a weak structure, it is a sure sign that the student did not
develop an outline—or even outline *after* drafting the paper. Without such
an outline, the essay may ramble on endlessly, and reading it becomes an
exercise in shaking hands with an octopus. In contrast, if you have a good
outline, you will find that the paper almost writes (or rewrites) itself. You
know where your ideas and sentences are heading, and it is more likely that
you will be able to adhere to the schedule you set yourself.

If done correctly, your outline will imply a logical progression of the
points of interest that you want to cover. You will be able to produce a parallel construction of the text and a balanced hierarchy of organization.
Initially, you can generate a tentative and general outline as you use the
library's resources to search for reference material to flesh out the paper
when the time comes to sit down and write. Use comparison and contrast as
a way of structuring the outline in your mind; then pull together facts or
studies to document and expand on your subtopics.

Some students find it difficult to begin making an outline. If you are
having a problem getting started, there are three tricks you can try:

◆ Think of the outline as a table of contents based on the  headings you
   might want to use.
◆ Shop around for an interesting quote that encourages fresh thinking
   and can later launch the introduction as well as capture and focus the
   reader's interest.

◆ Ask yourself the reporter's questions: *who, what, when, where,* and *why.*

Before you begin writing (discussed in Chapter 6), you will want to revise the preliminary outline so that it reflects the organizational structure you will use to shape the paper. This structure should be viewed not as carved in stone, but as something plastic that you can mold to your ideas as they continue to develop. Use the structure to guide you, but do not be afraid to change it if your thinking changes.

## Making Ideas Parallel

Outline items can be set down in topics, sentences, or paragraphs. The specific form you choose should be the only one used in the outline so that all the ideas are parallel. In the following outline fragment, based on Anne's paper in Appendix A, the ideas are clearly not parallel:

I. Introduction
   A. Two views of intelligence
      1. g-centric view—the general overriding factor of intelligence is measured by every task on an intelligence test
         a. Piaget
         b. Sternberg and Detterman
   B. Multiplex view
      1. What is Gardner's theory of "intelligences"?
   C. Seven kinds of intelligence

The problem with this abbreviated outline is that it is a hodgepodge of topics, idea fragments, questions, and so forth. Working with this jumble is like swimming upstream. Such an outline will only sabotage your efforts to put thoughts and notes into a logical sequence. Contrast this inconsistent structure with the parallel structure of the following outline as it covers the same points:

I. Two views of intelligence
   A. g-centric view
      1. Traditional approach
      2. Measures mathematical and linguistic skills
   B. Multiplex view
      1. Newer approach
      2. Goes beyond mathematical and linguistic skills

## Putting Ideas in Order

Whether you use topics, sentences, or paragraphs for your outline, group your information in descending order from the most general facts or ideas to the most specific details and examples. We see this approach clearly in the parallel format of the outline shown immediately above. The same rule applies whether you are outlining definitions and evaluation criteria or the nature of a specific theory that you plan to develop further in the first draft:

II. Gardner's theory of "intelligences"
   A. Definition of intelligence
      1. Problem-solving and creative abilities
      2. Evaluation criteria
         a. Isolated if brain-damaged
         b. Existence of exceptional populations
         c. Unique core operations
         d. Distinctive developmental history
         e. Existence of primitive antecedents
         f. Open to experimentation
         g. Predicts performance on tests
         h. Information content accessible
   B. Kinds of intelligence
      1. Logical-mathematical
      2. Linguistic
      3. Spatial
      4. Bodily-kinesthetic
      5. Musical
      6. Personal intelligences
         a. Intrapersonal
         b. Interpersonal

Another convention in making an outline is that there should be two or more subtopics under any topic, as illustrated in Exhibit 17. The use of roman numerals I, II, III; capitals A, B, C; arabic numerals 1, 2, 3; small letters a, b, c; and finally numbers and letters in parentheses serves as a means of classifying facts, ideas, and concepts. Thus, if you list I, you should list II; if A, then B; if 1, then 2; and so on.

The roman numerals indicate the outline's main ideas. Indented capital letters provide main divisions within each main idea. The letters and numbers that follow list the supporting details and examples. Note the indentation of each subtopic. Any category can be expanded to fit the number of supporting details or examples that you wish to cover in the paper. Any lapses in logic are bound to surface if you use this system of organization, and you can catch and correct them before proceeding.

For example, look at the following abbreviated outline; the entry labeled "B" is a conspicuous lapse in logic:

II. Gardner's theory of "intelligences"
   A. His definition of intelligence
   B. How did the concept of "g" originate?
   C. Seven kinds of intelligence

**EXHIBIT 17**   *Subdivision of the outline*

---

I.
  A.
  B.
    1.
    2.
      a.
      b.
        (1)
        (2)
          (a)
          (b)
II.

---

Item B should be moved from this section of the outline to that pertaining to g-centric views of intelligence. Some items may require a return to the library to clarify a point or to fill in with the appropriate reference material.

## Template for Writing and Note Taking

The outline is a way not only to organize your thoughts but also to make it easier to start writing. If you use the phrase or sentence format, the paper will almost write itself. We see this clearly by returning to a segment of the outline of Anne's paper:

II. Gardner's theory of "intelligences"
  A. Definition of intelligence
    1. ". . . the ability to solve problems, or to create products that are valued within one or more cultural settings" (Gardner, 1983, p. x)
    2. Intellectual talent must satisfy eight criteria (Gardner, 1983)
      a. Potential to isolate the intelligence by brain damage
      b. Existence of exceptional populations (savants) implying the distinctive existence of a special entity

Had the outline used complete sentences, the paper would write itself:

II. Gardner's theory of "intelligences"
  A. Definition of intelligence
    1. Gardner (1983) conceives of intelligence as "the ability to solve problems, or to create products that are valued within one or more cultural settings" (p. x).
    2. He argues that a talent must fit eight criteria to be considered "intelligence" (1983).

a. There is potential to isolate the intelligence by brain damage.
b. Exceptional populations (e.g., savants) provide evidence for distinct entities.

In Chapter 2, we alluded to one other helpful hint about using an outline. The outline's coding system makes it convenient to code the notes you take during your literature search in the library. If your notes refer to section "II.B.1." of your outline, then you would write this code on the card or photocopy. In this way, order is brought to your notes. If you spread them on a large table and sort through them according to the section of the outline that each note pertains to, then the paper will take shape from your notes and the outline, each component enhancing the other.

Keep in mind, however, that the outline is only a guide. Its form will probably change as you integrate your notes.

## Outlining After the Fact

Some students write their papers over a two-semester period (for example, an undergraduate thesis) and may feel they cannot outline from the outset because they do not know where the final research will go. When they *do* sit down to write, they tend to incorporate material from their earlier drafts, but they do not make an outline first. Still other students find the process of making an outline too exacting, preferring instead to sit at a word processor and let the stream of ideas flow spontaneously.

If either case describes you, then at least outline after the fact. To assure yourself that your work has an appealing, coherent form—what psychologists call a *good gestalt*—make a "table of contents" of your first draft and then do a more detailed outline within the headings and subheadings. Ask yourself:

◆ Is the discussion focused, and do the ideas flow from or build on one another?
◆ Is there ample development of each idea?
◆ Are there supporting details for each main idea discussed?
◆ Are the ideas balanced?
◆ Is the writing to the point, or have I gone off on a tangent?

An experienced writer working with a familiar topic can sometimes achieve success without a detailed outline. But for others, the results often create havoc and frustration, not to mention wasted time and effort. If you would like to practice on someone else's work, try outlining some section of Anne's paper. Ask yourself how well her discussion addresses the five preceding questions. If you find problems with the structure of her discussion, think of ways she could have avoided them or corrected them after the first draft.

# CHAPTER FIVE

# Planning the Research Report

All research reports have a structure whose core is qualitative
or quantitative data. The literature review usually involves only
a few key studies. This chapter describes the structure and
form of an experimental (quantitative) and an archival
(qualitative) research report, and it suggests ways to begin
organizing your thoughts. (If you are writing an essay, you
can skip this chapter and go on to Chapter 6.)

## The Basic Structure

Research methods texts routinely cover data collection and data analysis,
and we will assume that you are mastering the techniques they describe.
What remains is to develop a research report that will explain in clear language (a) what you did, (b) why you did it, (c) what you found out, (d) what
it means, and (e) what you concluded. Well-written reports imply a logical
progression in thought, and by adhering to the structure described in this
chapter, you can create this kind of order in your finished report.

Looking at Bruce's report (Appendix B) and Peter's report (Appendix C), we see that both have eight parts:

Title page
Abstract
Introduction
Method
Results
Discussion
References
Appendix(es)

Except for the layout of the title page and the addition of appendixes in
Bruce's and Peter's reports, the basic structure corresponds to a standard
reporting format that has evolved over many years in psychology. Later on,
we will discuss the layout of the paper (for example, the "page header" in
the upper right corner). You can see that the title page in the two reports is

straightforward, and therefore we can focus our attention on the remaining parts.

# Abstract

Although the abstract appears at the beginning of your report, it is actually written after you complete the rest of your paper. The abstract provides a concise summary of your report. Think of it as a distillation of the important points covered in the body of the report. Thus, in succinct paragraphs in the sample research reports, Bruce and Peter give synopses of what they did, what they found, and what they concluded.

When planning your abstract, answer these questions as concisely as possible:

◆ What was the objective or purpose of my research study?
◆ What principal method did I use?
◆ Who were the research participants?
◆ What were my major findings?
◆ What did I conclude from these findings?

More detailed and more specific statements about methods, results, and conclusions are given in the body of your report. The brief summary of the abstract lets the reader anticipate what your report is about. For another example of a research abstract, look at Susan Anthony's synopsis in Exhibit 12 (page 28).

# Introduction

The introduction provides the rationale for your research and prepares the reader for the methods you have chosen. Thus you should give a concise history and background of your topic, leading into your hypotheses or questions. For example, Bruce cites data that underscore the importance of his topic and then summarizes the relevant results of previous research on the topic. In this way, he develops a logical foundation for his hypotheses. Peter's report also begins with some background data and shows an appealing logical order that leads us directly into his hypotheses.

Your literature review should also show the development of your hypotheses or exploratory questions and the reason(s) you believe the research topic is worth studying. The strongest introductions are those that state the research problem or the hypotheses in such a way that the method section appears to be a natural consequence of that statement. If you can get readers to think when they later see your method section, "Yes, of course, that's what this researcher had to do to answer this question," then you will have succeeded in writing a strong introduction.

Here are some questions to ask yourself as you plan the introduction:

◆ What was the purpose of my study?
◆ What terms need to be defined?
◆ How does my study build on or derive from other studies?
◆ What were my working hypotheses or expectations?

# Method

The next step is to detail the methods and procedures used. If you used research participants, then you should describe them (for example, age, sex, and number of participants, as well as the way they were selected and any other details that will help to specify them). Psychologists are trained to ask questions about the generalizability of research results. Your instructor will be thinking about the generalizability of your findings across both persons and settings (that is, the *external validity* of results). For example, if your research participants were college students, then the instructor may ask whether your results can be generalized beyond this specialized population. (For an informative discussion of this problem, see D. O. Sears, "College Sophomores in the Laboratory: Influences of a Narrow Data Base on Social Psychology's View of Human Nature," *Journal of Personality and Social Psychology*, 1986, Vol. 51, pp. 515–530.)

Also included in this section should be a description of any tests or measures and the context in which they were used. Even if you used well-known, standardized tests (TAT, MMPI, or WAIS, for example), it is still a good idea to capsulize them in a few sentences. By describing them, you communicate to the reader that you understand the nature and purpose of the instruments you used.

For example, suppose you used the Self-Monitoring Scale (see M. Snyder, "Self Monitoring of Expressive Behavior," *Journal of Personality and Social Psychology*, 1974, Vol. 30, pp. 526–537). The instructor will expect you to have done a background search to learn more about this instrument, and you will probably have discovered that research has shown this test to consist of three different dimensions (see "An Analysis of the Self-Monitoring Scale," by S. R. Briggs, J. M. Cheek, and A. H. Buss, *Journal of Personality and Social Psychology*, 1980, Vol. 38, pp. 679–686). In your report, you might describe the test as follows:

Subjects were presented with Snyder's (1974) 25-item Self-

Monitoring Scale, which was designed to measure the extent

of self-observation and self-control guided by situational

cues to social appropriateness. Briggs, Cheek, and Buss

(1980) showed the multidimensional nature of this test, identifying three distinct factors that form internally consis-

tent subscales. The Extraversion Subscale was described by

Briggs et al. as tapping the respondent's chronic tendency to

be the center of attention in groups, to tell stories and

jokes, and so on. The Other-Directedness Subscale was de-

scribed as measuring the respondent's willingness to change

his or her behavior to suit others. The Acting Subscale was

described as assessing liking and being good at speaking and

entertaining.

However, suppose you need to report only the nature of a particular measure and not any follow-up inferences by other researchers. For example, suppose you used the Need for Cognition Scale (see J. T. Cacioppo and R. E. Petty, "The Need for Cognition," *Journal of Personality and Social Psychology*, 1982, Vol. 42, pp. 116–131). You can describe the measure as follows:

Subjects were presented with Cacioppo and Petty's (1982) Need

for Cognition Scale. This is an 18-item measure of the ten-

dency to engage in and enjoy thinking.

If you know something about the reliability and validity of the measure you chose, include this information as well (along with the appropriate citation).

# Results

In the next major section, describe your findings. You might plan to show the results in a table or figure, as in the sample reports. Do not make your instructor guess what you are thinking; label your table or figure fully, and discuss the data in the narrative of this section so that it is clear what they represent. It is not necessary to repeat the results from the table or figure in your narrative; simply tell what they mean.

Ask yourself the following questions as you structure your results section:

◆ What did I find?
◆ How can I say what I found in a careful, detailed way?
◆ Is what I am planning to say precise and to the point?
◆ Will what I have said be clear to the reader?
◆ Have I left out anything of importance?

This section should consist of a careful, detailed analysis that strikes a balance between being discursive and being falsely or needlessly precise:

◆ You are guilty of *false precision* when something inherently vague is presented in overly precise terms. Suppose you used a standard attitude measure in your research, and suppose the research participants responded on a 5-point scale from "strongly agree" to "strongly disagree." It would be falsely precise to report the means to a high number of decimal places, because your psychological measure was not that sensitive to slight variations in attitudes.

◆ You are guilty of *needless precision* when (almost without thinking about it) you report something much more exactly than the circumstances require. For example, reporting the weight of mouse subjects to six decimal places might be within the bounds of your measuring instrument, but the situation does not call for such exactitude.

Incidentally, a common mistake when reporting attitudinal scores based on labeled 5-point alternatives is to say that a "Likert scale" was used. Technically, a *Likert scale* (named after Rensis Likert, its inventor) implies that the measure was developed by a particular method (called *summated ratings*). But this is not what most researchers really mean when they say they used a Likert scale. Some researchers skirt this problem by using the term "Likert-type scale," by which they merely mean that the response alternatives were accompanied by phrases or by words (for example, "very favorable," "favorable," "neutral," "unfavorable," and "very unfavorable"), but they did not use the method of summated ratings to develop the scale. If this is all you mean, you should forget about calling it a Likert-type scale and simply say something like "The response scale ranged from 'very favorable' (1) to 'very unfavorable' (5)."

Another convention that many students find confusing is the way that $p$ levels are to be presented. For example, if someone stated that "$p = .00000007$," would this be a case of needless precision? Statisticians often recommend reporting a precise value if you are reporting the $p$ level, that is, reporting two digits after the initial zeros (for example, .064, .0071, .00011, .000092). However, for many purposes a single digit after the initial zeros will suffice. If you are looking up $p$ values in a statistical table, you may not have the option of reporting them precisely. Thus, it is also conventional to state only that $p$ was less than ($<$) or greater than ($>$) the particular column value in the statistical table.

## Discussion

In the discussion section, you will use the facts you have gathered to form a cohesive unit. A review of the introductory section is often helpful. Think about how you will discuss your research findings in light of your original hypotheses. Did serendipity (discussed in Chapter 2) play a role in your study? If so, detail the unexpected by-products and ideas.

Try to write "defensively" without being too blatant about it. That is, be your own devil's advocate and ask yourself what a skeptical reader might see as the other side of your argument or conclusion. In particular, look for shortcomings or critical inconsistencies, and anticipate the reader's reaction to them. If you cannot find any holes in your argument or conclusion, ask a clever friend to help you out.

Here are some additional questions to consider as you begin to structure this section:

- ◆ What was the purpose of my study?
- ◆ How do my results relate to that purpose?
- ◆ Did I make any serendipitous findings of interest?
- ◆ How valid and generalizable are my findings?
- ◆ Are there larger implications in these findings?
- ◆ Is there an alternative way to interpret my results?

You might plan a separate conclusions section if you feel more comfortable with that format or have a lot to cover that you would like to separate from the main body of your discussion. However, it is quite proper to treat the final paragraph or two of your discussion section as the conclusion. In either case, your conclusions should be stated as clearly and concisely as possible.

If there were larger implications, this would be the place to spell them out. Are there implications for further research? If so, suggest them here. For example, Bruce notes that one of his findings seemingly contradicted previous research, and he suggests some further research to reconcile the contradictory results. Peter points out the limited sample size of his study and also raises some ideas for further research.

## References

Once you have made plans for writing the body of the report, give some thought to your reference material again. You will need to include an alphabetized listing of all the sources of information from which you drew. To avoid retracing your steps in the library, keep a *running list* of the material that will appear in this section as you progress through the early preparation of the report. If you are using a word processor, then add each reference to the back of the report as you cite it in your narrative. If you are using the index-card method, make a separate card for each reference that you actually use in your report; it will be a simple matter later to alphabetize the cards and make sure that none have been omitted. It is essential that every citation also be listed in the references.

## Appendix

The purpose of this final section is to display the raw materials and computations of your investigation. For example, if you used a lengthy questionnaire or test (which cannot be adequately presented in the limited space of the method section), then include it in the appendix. Peter includes his coding sheet for raters in an "Appendix A." Many instructors like to see the student's calculations on the raw data, which Peter includes in an "Appendix B" and Bruce includes in a single appendix.

Your instructor may not require an appendix or may stipulate a different list of items to be included. Keep all of your notes and data until the instructor has returned your report and you have received a grade in the course, just in case the instructor has questions about your work.

## Organizing Your Thoughts

In the preceding chapter we described how to make an outline for the essay; the research report does not require a gross outline because its formal structure already provides a skeleton waiting to be fleshed out. Nevertheless, all researchers find it absolutely essential to organize their thoughts about each section before writing the first draft. There are three ways to do this:

- ◆ If you would like to learn about outlining, examine Chapter 3 for guidelines on how to outline before or after the fact.
- ◆ You can make notes on separate index cards for each major point (for example, the rationale of the study, the derivation of each hypothesis, and each background study) and draw on these notes to write your first draft.
- ◆ If you are using a word processor, you can simply make a file of such notes.

If you are still having a hard time getting going, here are two more tips:

- ◆ Imagine you are sitting across a table from a friend; tell your "friend" what you found.
- ◆ Take a pocket tape recorder for a walk; tell it what you found in your research.

No matter what approach you favor, make sure that your notes or files are accurate and complete. If you are summarizing someone else's study, then you must note the full citation. If you are quoting someone, include the statement in quotation marks and make sure that you have copied it exactly.

# CHAPTER SIX

# Writing and Revising

Writing a first draft is a little like taking the first dip in chilly ocean waters on a hot day. It may be uncomfortable at the outset but feels better once you get used to it. In this chapter, we provide some pointers to buoy you up as you begin writing. We also provide tips to help you revise your work.

## Concentrating on the Objective

At this stage of your work, you should have an ordered set of notes and an outline if you are writing an essay, or a given structure if your project is a research report. The notes you have assembled can be thought of as the bare bones of the paper. Sentences and paragraphs will be combined now to fill out the skeleton using the notes you collected. At this point, you must concentrate on your objective and decide which notes are relevant and which are superfluous. A recollection from B. F. Skinner's memoirs is relevant (see *Notebooks*, Prentice Hall, 1980).

Skinner told about the Collier brothers, who were found dead in a house that was completely filled with rubbish. They were possessed by an uncontrollable urge to save string, newspapers, and boxes and could never throw anything out. Skinner called them victims of "control by a worsening schedule" (p. 300), by which he meant that the reward they received from each new box, piece of string, or newspaper must have gradually diminished as the collection grew. They must have realized that outsiders would have to be brought in to clean up the mess, and that they would ridicule the Colliers.

It is not always easy to discard something we have made an effort to save, including studies and quotes that we have gone to the trouble to track down. But quantity should not replace quality and relevance in the notes you finally use in your research report or essay. Instructors are more impressed by tightly reasoned papers than by ones that are overflowing with superfluous material. It is best to approach the writing and revising stage with an open but focused mind, that is, a mind that focuses on the objective but is nevertheless open to discarding irrelevant material (not research data, however).

# The Self-Motivator Statement

To begin the first draft, write down somewhere for yourself the purpose or goal you have in mind (that is, what your paper will be about). Make this *self-motivator statement* succinct so that you have a focus for your thoughts as you begin to set them down on paper or enter them into a word processor.

If we refer to the three sample papers, we can imagine the following self-motivators:

### From Anne

My essay will contrast the traditional view of intelligence with Gardner's view, which illustrates what I will call the multiplex approach, and I will tell how he has answered his critics.

### From Bruce

I'm going to describe how I found that tipping increases when people are given a small gift, but that this effect is not simply due to reciprocity.

### From Peter

I found that children's books more often portray female characters as working in the household and male characters as working outside the home, and I will draw the implications of these findings for the perpetuation of gender-based stereotypes.

This trick of using a self-motivator statement can help to concentrate your thoughts and make the task of writing seem less formidable. The self-motivator is a good way simply to get you going and keep you clear-headed. You will be less apt to go off on a tangent if you remind yourself of exactly where you want your paper to go.

# The Opening

A good opening is crucial if you want to engage the reader's attention and interest. Some psychologists are masters at writing good openings, but most articles and books in this and related fields (as you discovered in your literature search) start out ponderously. There are enough cases of ponderous writing so that we need not give examples. But what about openings that grip our minds and make us want to delve further into the work?

One way to begin your paper in an inviting way is to pose a stimulating question. For example, Sissela Bok opened her book *Lying: Moral Choice in Public and Private Life* (Pantheon, 1978) with a number of questions:

> Should physicians lie to dying patients so as to delay the fear and anxiety which the truth might bring them? Should professors exaggerate the excellence of their students on recommendations in order to give them a better chance in a tight job market? Should parents conceal from children the fact that they were adopted? Should social scientists send investigators masquerading as patients to physicians in order to learn about racial and sexual biases in diagnosis and treatment? Should government lawyers lie to Congressmen who might otherwise oppose a much-needed welfare bill? And should journalists lie to those from whom they seek information in order to expose corruption? (p. xv)

Does this opening make you want to read further? Another technique is to impress on readers the paradoxical nature of a timely issue. In *Obedience to Authority* (Harper, 1969), Stanley Milgram began as follows:

> Obedience is as basic an element in the structure of social life as one can point to. Some system of authority is a requirement of all communal living, and it is only the man dwelling in isolation who is not forced to respond, through defiance or submission, to the commands of others. Obedience, as a determinant of behavior, is of particular relevance to our time. It has been reliably established that from 1933 to 1945 millions of innocent people were systematically slaughtered on command. Gas chambers were built, death camps were guarded, daily quotas of corpses were produced with the same efficiency as the manufacture of appliances. These inhumane policies may have originated in the mind of a single person, but they could only have been carried out on a massive scale if a very large number of people obeyed orders. (p. 1)

The passage above was written before there were concerns about sexist language: Milgram's use of the word *man* ("it is only the man dwelling in isolation") as a general term for men and women is now considered improper usage. Instead, he could have said "people dwelling in isolation" (we return to this issue later). However, perhaps you are thinking "What does Milgram's or Bok's work have to do with me? These are Ph.D. psychologists who were writing for publication, but I'm just writing a paper for a course." The answer any instructor will give you is that an expectation of good writing is not limited to published work (for example, business correspondence, company memos, applications for jobs).

What makes the opening paragraphs of the three sample papers inviting? Each strikes a resonant chord in the reader. There are many other useful opening techniques: a definition, an anecdote, a metaphor that compares or contrasts, an epigraph (an opening quotation), and so on—all of these are devices that a writer can use to shape a beginning paragraph. Not only should it draw the reader into the work, but it should also serve to provide momentum for the writer as her or his words and ideas begin to flow. Anne begins her paper by pointing up a paradox, which is that we speak of "intelligence" in many different ways, but psychologists have traditionally viewed it in one general way. Bruce and Peter start with some interesting facts, which immediately draw us into the logic of their introductions.

## Settling Down to Write

Should you find yourself still having trouble beginning the introductory paragraph, try the trick of not starting at the opening of your paper. Start writing whatever section you feel will be the easiest, and then tackle the rest as your ideas begin to flow. When faced with the blank page or blank computer screen and flashing cursor, some students escape by taking a nap, watching MTV, surfing the Net, or checking their E-mail. Recognize these counterproductive moves for what they are, because they can drain your energies. Use them instead as rewards *after* you have done a good job of writing.

The following are general pointers to ensure that your writing will go as smoothly as possible:

◆ While writing, try to work in a quiet, well-lighted place in two-hour stretches (dim lighting makes people sleepy).

◆ Go for a walk by yourself to collect your thoughts and to think of a sentence to get you going again (the fresh air will also be invigorating).

◆ If you are typing your first draft, double- or triple-space it so you will have room for legible revisions. If you are writing on a notepad, skip a line for each line you write down. If you are using a word processor, modify the system format to double-space your printout.

◆ Be sure to number the pages you write because it is maddening to mix up unnumbered pages. If you are using a word processor, modify the system format so the page numbers will automatically appear as shown in the sample papers.

◆ When you take a break, try to stop at a point that is midway through an idea or a paragraph. In this way you can resume work where you left off and avoid feeling stuck or having to start cold. You might also add a phrase or some notes that will get you back on track once you return to your writing.

◆ Try to pace your work with time to spare so that you can complete the first draft and let it rest for 24 hours. When you return to the completed first draft after a night's sleep, your critical powers will be enhanced, and you will have a fresh approach to shaping the final draft.

# Ethics of Writing and Reporting

Several years ago, the American Psychological Association revised its ethical principles for professional psychologists (see *American Psychologist,* December 1992) to include guidelines for authors. Some of these standards also have implications for students who are writing papers, for example:

• Psychologists are responsible for making available the data on which their conclusions are based. The implication for students writing research reports is that they also are expected to produce all of their raw data as required by the instructor.

• It is unethical to misrepresent original research by publishing it in more than one journal and implying that each report represents a different study. The implication for students is that it is also unethical to submit the same work for additional credit in different courses.

• Authors are expected to give credit where it is due. The implication for a student is that if someone gave you an idea, you should credit that person in a footnote.

The most fundamental ethical principle in science is honesty in all aspects of the research. An old Bohemian legend tells of an archer who is offered an empire to teach the king to become a great marksman. One day, the king comes upon the archer standing next to a grove of trees, and each tree has a chalked circle and an arrow in the exact center of the circle. The king is greatly impressed, but the honest archer says, "Keep your empire, for the secret of my skill is that I shoot first and draw the circle afterward." The relevance of this fable is to be equally honest when describing all your hypotheses. Do not falsely represent those developed *after* you have seen the data as hypotheses developed at the *outset.* Always make clear which came first—the "circle" or the "arrow."

# Avoiding Plagiarism

Being honest and accurate also means never plagiarizing, even accidentally. The term *plagiarism,* which comes from a Latin word meaning "kidnapper," refers to stealing another person's ideas or work and passing them off as your own. Two informative books on this subject are T. Mallon's *Stolen Words: Forays into the Origins and Ravages of Plagiarism* (Penguin, 1991) and M. C. LaFollette's *Stealing into Print: Fraud, Plagiarism, and Misconduct in Scientific Publishing* (University of California Press, 1992). It is crucial that you understand what constitutes plagiarism and what are its consequences for those who commit it. Plagiarism in student writing is often accidental, but it is important to avoid "kidnapping" someone else's work even unintentionally. For students, the penalties for plagiarism in a class assignment or a thesis may be severe.

This warning does not mean that you cannot use other people's ideas or work in your writing. What it does mean is that you must give the author of that material full credit for originality and not misrepresent (intentionally or accidentally) that material as your own original work. To illustrate, suppose a student submitted an essay containing the following passage:

```
Deceit and violence are two forms of deliberate assault on
human beings. Both can coerce people into acting against
their will. Most harm that can happen to people through vio-
lence can also happen to them through deceit. However,
deceit controls more subtly, because it works on belief as
well as action. Even Othello, whom few would have dared to
try to subdue by force, could be brought to destroy himself
and Desdemona through falsehood.
```

Sounds like an A paper? Yes, but the student would receive an F in the course. The reason for the student's failure is plagiarism. The student stole the passage out of Sissela Bok's work. In *Lying: Moral Choice in Public and Private Life*, Bok states:

> Deceit and violence—these are the two forms of deliberate assault on human beings. Both can coerce people into acting against their will. Most harm that can befall victims through violence can come to them also through deceit. But deceit controls more subtly, for it works on belief as well as action. Even Othello, whom few would have dared to try to subdue by force, could be brought to destroy himself and Desdemona through falsehood. (p. 18)

How might the student have used Bok's work without falling into plagiarism? The answer is to put quotes around the material you want to copy verbatim—and then give a complete citation. Even if you just wanted to paraphrase the work, you are still responsible for giving full credit to the original author. A reasonable paraphrase might appear as follows:

```
Bok (1978) makes the case that deceit and violence "both can
coerce people into acting against their will" (p. 18).
Deceit, she notes, controls more subtly, because it affects
belief. Using a literary analogy, she observes, "Even
Othello, whom few would have dared to try to subdue by
```

force, could be brought to destroy himself and Desdemona through falsehood" (p. 18).

## Lazy Writing

Some lazy students, on hearing that quotations and citations are not construed by definition as plagiarism, submit papers saturated with quoted material. Unless you feel it absolutely essential, avoid quoting long passages throughout a paper. It may be necessary to quote or paraphrase some material (with a citation, of course), but your written work is expected to result from your own individual effort. Quoting a simple sentence that can easily be paraphrased signals lazy writing.

In other words, your paper should reflect *your* thoughts on a particular topic after you have carefully examined and synthesized material from the sources you feel are pertinent. The penalty for lazy writing is not as severe as that for plagiarism, although often it means a reduced grade. Avoid both problems: plagiarism and lazy writing. As noted earlier, it is a good idea to keep your note cards, outlines, and rough drafts, because instructors will ask students for such material if a question arises about the originality of their work.

And finally, many students use terms that they do not understand, especially when dealing with technical material—anatomical or statistical terms, for example. Although this is not considered plagiarism, it does constitute lazy writing (and bad scholarship as well). Always try to make your point in your own words. If someone else has said it much better than you can ever hope to say it, quote (and cite) or paraphrase (and cite) the other source. On the other hand, if you really cannot say it in your own words, then you do not understand it well enough to write about it.

## Tone

As you write, there are certain basic style points to keep in mind. The *tone* of your paper refers to the manner in which you express your ideas to the reader. Your writing should not be dull; presumably you are writing on a topic that you find fascinating, inasmuch as you chose it.

Here are some hints on how to create the right tone:

◆ Strive for an explicit, straight-forward, interesting but not emotional way of expressing your thoughts, findings, and conclusions.
◆ Avoid having your essay or research report read like a letter to a favorite aunt ("Here's what Jones and Smith say . . ." or "So I told the research participants . . .").
◆ Do not try to duplicate a journalist's slick style, familiar in the glib spoken reports on network TV and in supermarket tabloids.

◆ It is all right to use the first person ("I shall discuss . . ." or "My con-clusion is that . . ."). But do not refer to yourself as *we* unless you have multiple personality disorder and "all of you" collaborated on the paper.

◆ Strive for an objective, direct tone that keeps your reader subordi-nate to the material you are presenting. Do not write: "The reader will note that the results were. . . ." Instead, write: "The results were. . . ."

◆ A famous writing manual is *The Elements of Style* (Prentice Hall, 1979), by W. Strunk, Jr., and E. B. White. One of Professor Strunk's admoni-tions is: "Omit needless words. Omit needless words. Omit needless words."

## Nonsexist Language

The question of *word gender* has become a matter of some sensitivity among many writers, particularly in psychology and related areas. One reason to discourage sex bias in written and spoken communication is that words can influence people's thoughts and deeds, and we do not want to reinforce stereotypes or prejudiced behaviors. To be sure, there is sometimes a good reason not to use gender-free pronouns. Suppose a new drug has been tested only on male subjects. If the researchers used only gender-free pro-nouns when referring to their participants, a reader might mistakenly infer that the results apply to both sexes.

The point, of course, is to think before you write. In her book *The Elements of Nonsexist Usage* (Prentice Hall, 1990), Val Dumond made the fol-lowing observation concerning overuse of the word *man*: "When the word is used, that is the mental picture that is formed. The picture is what simul-taneously represents a conceptual meaning to the interpreter. Since a female picture does not come to mind when the word *man* is used, it would follow that man does not represent in any way a female human" (p. 1).

When the issues of sexist language first gained prominence in psychol-ogy, researchers and others often used contrived words such as *s/he* and *he/she* to avoid sexist language. Experienced writers and editors have pro-posed various ways to circumvent the awkwardness of such forms and also the possible trap of gender-biased language. In general, beware of mascu-line nouns and pronouns that will give a sex bias to your writing. There are two simple rules:

◆ Use plural pronouns when you are referring to both genders, for instance, "They did . . ." instead of "He did . . ."; and ". . . to them" instead of ". . . to him."

◆ Use masculine and feminine pronouns if the situation calls for them. For example, if the study you are discussing used only male research participants, then the masculine pronouns are accurate. The forms *he/she* and *s/he* are not only awkward but in this case would mislead the reader into thinking that the research participants were both women and men.

# Voice

The verb forms you use in your writing can speak with one of two voices: active or passive. You write in the *active voice* when you represent the subject of your sentence as performing the action expressed by your verb ("The research participants responded by . . ."). You write in the *passive voice* when the subject of your sentence undergoes the action expressed by your verb ("The response made by the research participant was . . .").

If you try to rely mainly on the active voice, you will have a more vital, compelling style:

### Active Voice (Good)

```
Dollard and Miller hypothesized that frustration leads to
aggression.
```

### Passive Voice (Not as Good)

```
It was hypothesized by Dollard and Miller that frustration
leads to aggression.
```

# Verb Tense

The verb tenses you use in your paper can get into a tangle unless you observe the following basic rules:

- ◆ Use the *past tense* to report studies that were done in the past ("Jones and Smith found . . ."). If you are writing a research report, then both method and results sections can usually be written in the past tense because your study has already been accomplished ("In this study, data *were* collected . . ." and "In these questionnaires, there *were* . . .").
- ◆ Use the *present tense* to define terms ("Multiplex, in this context, *refers* to . . ." and "A stereotype *is* defined as . . ."). The present tense is also frequently used to state a general hypothesis or to make a general claim ("Gardner *theorizes* that there are multiple intelligences . . .").
- ◆ The *future tense* can be saved for the section of your paper in which you discuss implications for further investigation ("Future research *will be* necessary . . ."), but it is not essential to use the future tense. You could say, "Further investigation *is* warranted. . . ."

# Agreement of Subject and Verb

Make sure each sentence expresses a complete thought and has a *subject* (in general terms, something that performs the action) and a *verb* (an action that is performed or a state of being).

### Subject and Verb Agree

```
The participants [subject] were [verb] students. . . .
```

Because the subject is plural (*participants*), the verb form used (*were*) is also plural. This means the verb and subject agree, a basic rule of grammar.

In most sentence forms, achieving this agreement is a simple matter. But trouble can sometimes arise, so here are some tips:

◆ When you use *collective nouns* (those that name a group), they can be either singular or plural, for example, *committee, team, faculty*. When you think of the group as a single unit, use a singular verb ("The union *is* ready to settle . . ."). Plurals are called for when you want to refer to the components of a group ("The faculty *were* divided on the issue . . .").

◆ Trouble can pop up when words come between subject and verb: "Therapy [*singular subject*], in combination with behavioral organic methods of weight gain, exemplifies [*singular verb form*] this approach." It would be incorrect to write: "Therapy, in combination with behavioral organic methods of weight gain, *exemplify* [*plural verb form*] this approach.

◆ Use a *singular verb form* after the following: *each, either, everyone, someone, neither, nobody*. Here is a correct usage: "When everyone is ready, the experiment will begin."

# Common Usage Errors

Instructors see frequent usage errors in student papers. The inside front cover of this manual lists pairs of words that are both pronounced similarly (*homonyms*) and often confused with one another, such as *accept* ("receive") and *except* ("other than").

Another pair of confusing homonyms is *affect* and *effect*. In their most common form, the words *effect*, a noun meaning "outcome" (as in "Aggression is often an *effect* of frustration"), and *affect*, a verb meaning "to influence" (as in "Frustration *affects* how a person behaves"), are frequently confused. Moreover, *effect* can also be a verb meaning "to bring about" (as in "The procedure *effected* a measurable improvement"), and in psychology, *affect* can be a noun meaning "emotion" (as in "Subjects may show a positive *affect*").

Another potential source of problems is the incorrect use of the singular and plural of some familiar terms, for instance:

| *Singular* | *Plural* |
|---|---|
| analysis | analyses |
| anomaly | anomalies |
| appendix | appendixes or appendices (both are correct) |
| criterion | criteria |
| datum | data |
| hypothesis | hypotheses |
| phenomenon | phenomena |
| stimulus | stimuli |

For example, one common usage error is the confusion of *phenomena* [*plural term*] with *phenomenon* [*singular term*]. It would be incorrect to write "This [*singular pronoun*] phenomena [*plural subject*] is [*singular verb*] of interest." The correct form is either "This phenomenon is . . ." or "These phenomena are . . ."

Another common error results from the confusion of *data* [*plural term*] with *datum* [*singular term*]. It would be incorrect to write "The data [*plural subject*] indicates [*singular verb*]. . . ." The correct form is "The data indicate. . . ."

One common source of confusion is in the misuse of the words *between* and *among*. As a general rule, use *between* when you are referring to two items only; use *among* when there are more than two items. For example, it would be incorrect to write "between the three of them."

There is, however, one anomaly that you can do nothing about correcting. In the analysis of variance (called *ANOVA*), conventional usage says "between sum of squares" and the "between mean square," even if the number of conditions being compared is more than two.

Other common problems concern the use of some *prefixes* in psychological terms:

◆ The prefix *inter-* means "between" (for example, *interpersonal* means "between persons"); the prefix *intra-* means "within" (for example, *intrapersonal* means "within the person").

◆ The prefix *intro-* means "inward" or "within"; the prefix *extra-* means "outside" or "beyond." The psychological term *introverted* thus refers to an "inner-directed personality"; the term *extraverted* indicates an "outer-directed personality."

◆ The prefix *hyper* means "too much"; the prefix *hypo-* means "too little." Hence, the term *hypothyroidism* refers to a deficiency of thyroid hormone, while *hyperthyroidism* denotes an excess of thyroid hormone, and a *hyperactive* child is one who is excessively active.

# Punctuation

The correct use of the various punctuation marks will help prevent confusion in your writing. A *period* ends a declarative sentence. It also follows an abbreviation, as in the following common abbreviations of Latin words:

| | |
|---|---|
| cf. | from *confer* ("compare") |
| e.g. | from *exempli gratia* ("for example") |
| et al. | from *et alia* ("and others") |
| et seq. | from *et sequens* ("and following") |
| ibid. | from *ibidem* ("in the same place") |
| i.e. | from *id est* ("that is") |
| op. cit. | from *opere citato* ("in the work cited") |
| viz. | from *videlicet* ("namely") |

If you continually write *eg.* or *et. al.* in your paper, you will be telling the instructor, "I don't know the meaning of these terms!" The reason, of course, is that *e.g.* is the abbreviation for two words, not one; *eg.* announces that you believe it is the abbreviation of one word. Putting a period after *et* tells the instructor that you believe it is an abbreviation, which it is not; it is an entire word.

On the subject of abbreviations, some others that you may encounter in the library are the short forms of English words:

| | |
|---|---|
| anon. | for *anonymous* |
| ch. | for *chapter* |
| diagr. | for *diagram* |
| ed. | for *editor* or *edition* |
| fig. | for *figure* |
| ms. | for *manuscript* |
| p. | for *page* |
| pp. | for *pages* |
| rev. | for *revised* |
| vol. | for *volume* |

The various uses of the *comma* include the following:

◆ Use commas to separate three or more items in a series ("Smith, Jones, and Brown" or "high, medium, and low scorers").

◆ Use commas to set off introductory phrases in a sentence ("In another experiment performed 10 years later, the same researchers found . . .").

◆ Use commas to set off thoughts or phrases that are incidental to or that qualify the basic idea of the  sentence ("This variable, although not part of the researchers' central hypothesis, was also examined . . .").

◆ Put a comma before connecting words (*and, but, or, nor, yet*) when they join independent clauses ("The subject lost weight, but he was still able to . . .").

The *semicolon* (;) is used to join independent clauses in a sentence when connecting words are omitted. A semicolon is called for when the thoughts in the two independent clauses are close, and the writer wishes to emphasize this point or to contrast the two thoughts:

### Semicolon for Connecting Thoughts

```
Anorexia nervosa is a disorder in which the victims liter-

ally starve themselves; despite their emaciated appearance,

they consider themselves overweight.
```

In most instances these long sentences can be divided into shorter ones, which will be clearer:

### No Semicolon

```
Anorexia nervosa is a disorder in which the victims liter-

ally starve themselves. Despite their emaciated appearance,

they consider themselves overweight.
```

Use a *colon* (:) to indicate that a list will follow, or to introduce an amplification. The colon tells the reader, "Note what follows":

### Colon to Indicate That a List Follows

```
Subjects were given the following items: (a) four calling

birds, (b) three French hens, (c) two turtle doves . . .
```

### Colon to Introduce an Amplification

Examples of this particular use of the colon are the titles of Anne's, Bruce's, and Peter's papers. Another example would be:

```
Gardner postulated two forms of the personal intelligences:

interpersonal and intrapersonal intelligence.
```

# Quotations

*Double quotation marks* (" ") are used to enclose direct quotations in the narrative of the paper, and *single quotation marks* (' ') indicate a quote within a quote:

## Quotation Marks

Subject B responded, "My feeling about this difficult situation was summed up in a nutshell by Jim when he said, 'It's a tough job, but somebody has to do it.' "

Here are more rules about punctuation when using quotations in your paper:

◆ If the appropriate punctuation is a comma or a period, it is included *within* the quotation marks.
◆ Colons and semicolons always come *after* the closing quotation marks.
◆ When the quotation is 40 or more words, it is set off from the body of the prose by means of indented margins, and quotation marks are omitted.

## Passage Containing Lengthy Quotation and Internal Quotation

What practical implications did Rosenthal and Jacobson (1968) draw from their research findings? They wrote:

As teacher-training institutions begin to teach the possibility that teachers' expectations of their pupils' performance may serve as self-fulfilling prophecies, there may be a new expectancy created. The new expectancy may be that children can learn more than had been believed possible, an expectation held by many educational theorists, though for quite different reasons. . . . The new expectancy, at the very least, will make it more difficult when they encounter the educationally disadvantaged for teachers to think, "Well, after all, what can you expect?" The man on the street may be permitted his opinions and prophecies of the unkempt children loitering in a dreary schoolyard. The teacher in the schoolroom may need to learn that those same prophecies within her may be fulfilled; she is no

```
casual passer-by. Perhaps Pygmalion in the classroom is

more her role. (pp. 181-182)
```

Notice that the quotation begins, "As teacher-training institutions . . ." and ends ". . . in the classroom is more her role"; the page numbers on which this passage appears in Rosenthal and Jacobson's book are shown in parentheses at the end.

This passage (like that by Milgram, quoted previously) was written before there were concerns about the question of assigning gender, and the authors referred to "the man on the street" and to the teacher as "she." If you wished to make the point that the quoted passage ignores gender, then you might insert in brackets the word *sic* (Latin, meaning "thus," denoting that a word or phrase that appears strange or incorrect has been quoted verbatim). The two sentences would then look like this:

```
The man [sic] on the street may be permitted his opinions

and prophecies of the unkempt children loitering in a dreary

schoolyard. The teacher in the schoolroom may need to learn

that those same prophecies within her [sic] may be ful-

filled; she is no casual passer-by.
```

Note that we did not insert *sic* after every gender term in the quoted passage. In the first sentence, the masculine pronoun *his* was not set off by *sic* because the referent is "man on the street." In the second sentence, the feminine pronoun *she* is also not set off, because the referent is "within her."

## Revising

In the next chapter, we consider the details of assembling and producing your final draft. Whether you are using a word processor or a typewriter, *revising* the first draft of your paper is best done after you have been able to leave the material entirely. When you approach your writing after having taken such a break (ideally, 24 hours or more), your critical powers will be sharper. Syntax errors, lapses in logic, and other problems will become evident, so that smoothing out these sections will be a relatively simple chore.

As you reread, consider the following do's and don'ts:

- ◆ Be concise.
- ◆ Break up long paragraphs that contain a lot of disparate ideas into smaller, more coherent paragraphs.
- ◆ Be specific.
- ◆ Choose words for what they mean, not just for how they sound.
- ◆ Double-check punctuation.
- ◆ Don't use a long word when a short one will do.

◆ Don't be redundant (for example, "most unique" is redundant).
◆ Don't let spelling errors mar your writing.

It is painfully difficult to revise when a word processor is not available. But if a typewriter is what you have, equip yourself with scissors and glue (retractable stick glue is the easiest to use). With these tools, rearranging paragraphs, condensing sentences, and adding or subtracting references will be less painful. Of course, the least painful option is to use a word processor.

## Using a Word Processor

If you are working with a word processor, you know that the steps involved in first drafts, revisions, and final drafts are telescoped. These stages lose their formal definition because the computer allows you, with the stroke of a key or the click of a mouse, to shift or change words, sentences, paragraphs, and even entire sections as you compose. Notes, long quotations, references, tables, and figures can be stored in the computer's memory or on a disk and retrieved as needed. A word processor releases the writer from an enormous amount of drudgery, even though it is not a substitute for the hard work of organizing ideas, thinking them through, and expressing them clearly.

Good word-processing programs also contain a dictionary (actually, a word inventory) that allows you to monitor your spelling of common English words. It can be very useful, but it can also lull students into a false sense of security. Many terms that psychologists and other professionals use may not appear in your word-processing inventory. A simple way to deal with this problem is to add unusual terms as you come across them. Start by adding the terms that appear inside the front and back covers of this manual. You will discover other relevant terms as you go about your literature search; keep a list, and then enter them into your system when you have a free moment.

If you are new to word processing (or are learning a new word-processing program), be sure you know how to save and back up your work when you are ready to start composing. A good system will do this for you automatically at regular intervals, but you must specify the interval you want. It is a good idea to save and back up at least every hour. You never know when the electricity will suddenly go out or someone will playfully or accidentally hit a wrong key, sending your work into oblivion. Making a "backup" means not only storing something inside the computer's hard drive (that is, if it's *your* PC) but also copying it onto a disk. Our habit is also to make a printout (called a hard copy) at the end of the day. Having a printed copy will allow you to inspect and modify the final layout to make sure it looks the way you want it to. It also allows you to polish your writing in a format that is tangible. Sometimes spelling errors and murky passages that are less apparent on-screen jump out as your eye traverses a printed page.

# CHAPTER SEVEN

# Layout and Production

This chapter provides you with general guidelines and tips for producing a finished product. The layout and production of your final draft are like the icing on a cake. If the underlying structure is sound, the result will be smooth and predictable.

## The First Impression

There are still students who use a typewriter or who hire a typist to prepare the final draft, but the most efficient way to write and to revise is to use a computer with a word-processing program. We used a serviceable, but pale-olithic, word processor in writing this manual, and even it has advantages that writing by hand or with a typewriter lacks. The most basic advantage is that you can cut out material from one section and easily paste it into another with just the touch of some keys or the movement of a mouse. But whether you are using a word processor, writing on a yellow pad, or using a typewriter, you need to be concerned about the appearance of your printed report or essay, because you never get a second chance to make a first impression.

We will start with an exaggerated illustration that only the most careless student would submit. Study the sample passage at the top of Exhibit 18. If you were the instructor and a student submitted a paper to you that began with this paragraph, what would your first impression be? How many problems do you count?

Corrected typographical error: *Pygmaliom*
Spelling mistake: *Jacobsen* (twice)
Usage error: *phenomena*
Corrected omission: *statistically significant*
Spelling mistake: *surpased*
Usage error: *&*
Typographical error: *inthe*
Spelling mistake: *intellectule*

If you were using a word processor with a "grammar check" and a "spell check," the program would catch some mistakes and prompt you to

**EXHIBIT 18    Appearance counts!**

---

In Pygmaliom [n] in the Classroom, Rosenthal and Jacobsen (1968) concluded that the phenomena of the self-fulfilling prophecy is as viable in the classroom as Rosenthal and his coworkers previously showed it to be in the scientist's laboratory. Students whose names were randomly selected and who were represented to be "bloomers" showed [statistically significant] IQ gains that surpased those of students not so labeled for their teachers. It was the label, Rosenthal & Jacobsen asserted, which created false positive expectations in the teachers' minds and, in turn, resulted in this difference in intellectule performance.

---

In Pygmalion in the Classroom, Rosenthal and Jacobson (1968) concluded that the phenomenon of the self-fulfilling prophecy is as viable in the classroom as Rosenthal and his coworkers previously showed it to be in the scientist's laboratory. Students whose names were randomly selected and who were represented to be "bloomers" showed statistically significant IQ gains that surpassed those of students not so labeled for their teachers. It was the label, Rosenthal and Jacobson asserted, which created false positive expectations in the teachers' minds and, in turn, resulted in this difference in intellectual performance.

---

correct them. But even the best word-processing programs are not infallible; they still miss mistakes because they do not recognize certain stylistic requirements that may have been violated. Previously, we advised you to make a backup hard copy (printout), which allows you to evaluate and polish the actual layout of the anticipated finished product. However, the printout may look deceptively clean, so do not be captivated by the finished look of the printed page. Check it carefully for errors of omission, stylistic mistakes, and lapses in logic.

With relatively little effort the top paragraph in Exhibit 18 could have been cleaned up to enhance the student's finished product. Compare the messy paragraph with the carefully edited and cleanly prepared version below it to see what a difference in initial impression the two paragraphs create.

# General Pointers

We assume (as your instructor does) that you will correct spelling mistakes, usage errors, and omissions before you submit your paper. What follows are general pointers as you set about producing the final product:

◆ Whether you are using a printer or a typewriter to produce the final manuscript, make sure the type is legible. If it is faint, invest in a new cartridge or ribbon.

◆ Use 8¹/₂ × 11 white paper. If you are typing the paper, use bond, not onionskin paper or "erasable" paper.

◆ Use double line spacing, and print or type on only one side of the paper, numbering pages in the upper-right corner as the sample papers illustrate.

◆ Make a second copy of the finished paper. The original is for your instructor, and the duplicate copy will ensure the immediate availability of an exact spare copy in case of an unforeseen problem.

◆ If you do not have access to a laser or an ink-jet printer but must use a daisy-wheel printer, use the strikeover (or letter-quality) mode rather than the first-draft mode to print your final copy.

◆ If you are using a word processor, it is okay to let the right margin remain ragged (uneven). That is, you do not need to use a justified right margin, which creates a block effect and, sometimes, odd spacing within lines.

◆ Use generous margins to leave space for the instructor to make comments. When typing, set your pica typewriter at 55 characters per line; on an elite, use 66 per line.

We turn now to other specifics of layout and processing (or typing) that will help to give your finished product an inviting appearance.

# Title Page Format

Glance at the title pages of the sample papers. The title summarizes the main idea of the project and is centered on the page. A good title is succinct and yet adequately describes to the reader the gist of the work. You will already have arrived at a working title when you narrowed your topic and drafted a proposal (Chapter 3). That title can now be changed or made more specific if you feel it is no longer accurate or completely descriptive of the finished project.

Other information is also shown on the title page of these sample papers:

The student's name (called the *byline*)

The number and name of the course or sequence for which the paper
was written

The date the paper will be submitted

It is optional to show the instructor's name (if the paper is submitted for a
course) or the adviser's name (if the paper is submitted to fulfill some other
requirement, such as a thesis). If the paper is a thesis, you should include an
acknowledgment page (after the title page) on which you thank your
adviser and any others who extended a helping hand as you worked on
your project. Incidentally, theses also usually include a table of contents
page.

Notice that the page number in the upper-right corner is accompanied
(on every page) by one or more words. These words are called *page headers*,
and their purpose is to make it easy for the reader to identify each manuscript page if any pages become separated. This is a convention recommended by the APA publication manual, and we think it is a good idea.
However, if you cannot figure out how to get your word processor to insert
a page header on every page, forget about it, and just include page numbers
and staple the manuscript.

Some instructors insist that papers for courses use title pages identical
to those on manuscripts submitted to journals. In that case, you really *will*
need to include the page header. Exhibit 19 recasts the title page of Bruce's
research paper as if it were being prepared for publication. The "running
head" is an abbreviated title that is printed at the top of the pages of a published article in some journals. The APA rule is that running heads cannot
exceed 50 characters, counting letters, punctuation, and spaces between
words. On the title page, the running head is placed at the left margin (flush
left) and is typed in capital letters. The title of Bruce's required paper in
Appendix B would be far too wordy for a journal submission, and Exhibit
19 shows how it might be shortened. The byline and affiliation are centered
beneath the title of the paper.

# Headings

It is customary to break up the text of a manuscript with headings. You can
derive these from the outline of your essay or, in the case of the research
report, use the headings that are inherent in the structure of the report
("Introduction," "Method," and so on). Incidentally, if you were submitting
your paper to a journal, you would not start the paper with a center heading because the "Introduction" is presumed to be implicit. However, we
recommend using this center heading as a reminder of the purpose of this
section.

Note how Anne's headings and subheadings lend symmetry to her
paper, showing its progressive development in concise phrases:

**EXHIBIT 19    Cover page of Bruce's paper in APA format**

```
                                                          Tipping   1


        Running head: RESTAURANT TIPPING



           Effect of an After-Meal Mint on Restaurant Tipping

                           Bruce Rind
                           Affiliation
```

Introduction

<u>Two Views of Intelligence</u>

<u>The g-centric View</u>

<u>The Multiplex View</u>

Gardner's Theory of "Intelligences"

<u>Definition of Intelligence</u>

<u>Seven Kinds of Intelligence</u>

<u>Independence of Abilities</u>

Criticisms of Multiplex Theories

<u>Nontraditional Orientation</u>

<u>Structure and Amenability to Tests</u>

Conclusions

Anne's paper uses two formats of headings: center and flush left. The *center heading* is used to separate the manuscript into major sections, is written in uppercase and lowercase letters, and is not underlined. To subdivide the major sections, she uses *subheadings* placed at the left margin (flush left), underlined, and in uppercase and lowercase. If we wished to use another level of subheadings, they would be indented, underlined, and followed by a period, with the body of the text immediately following the heading, for example:

<u>Seven Kinds of Intelligence</u>

    <u>Logical-Mathematical</u>. One traditional type of intelligence, called logical-mathematical by Gardner, refers to. . . . .

# Underlining

As this example shows, *underlining* can be used to distinguish levels of headings. Conventional usage also calls for the titles of books mentioned in the body of the text to be underlined ("In <u>Pygmalion in the Classroom,</u> Rosenthal and Jacobson...."). Underlining is also used in several other ways:

• Letters used as statistical symbols are underlined: $\underline{F}$, $\underline{N}$, $\underline{n}$, $\underline{P}$, $\underline{p}$, $\underline{t}$, $\underline{Z}$, and so forth. The purpose of this underlining is to indicate that the symbols should be italicized when they are printed. It can be a nuisance to underline formulaic symbols, and so if your instructor approves, then it is also acceptable to simply italicize the symbols if that is more convenient (for example, *F, N, n, P, p, t, Z*).

- Note that some symbols are in lowercase, and this can be very important. For example, avoid capitalizing t̲ if you mean Student's t̲ test, because a capital letter implies a quite different statistic.
- However, Greek letters used as statistical symbols are not underlined, for example, the symbol for chi-square ($\chi^2$), the symbol telling us to sum a set of scores ($\Sigma$), the symbol for the standard deviation of a set of scores ($\sigma$), or the symbol for the variance of a set of scores ($\sigma^2$).
- In reference lists, volume numbers of journal articles and titles of books and journals are underlined.
- Words that you wish to emphasize are underlined, but this should be done sparingly ("Effective teaching, the authors assert, will come only from the teachers' firm belief that their pupils c̲a̲n̲ perform . . .").

## Citations in Text

There are several simple conventions for citing an author's work in the narrative of a paper. The purpose of a citation is to make it easy for the reader to identify the source of a quotation or idea and then to locate the particular reference in the list at the end of the paper. The author-date method is the format recommended by the APA publication manual. The surname of the author and the year of publication are inserted in the narrative text at the appropriate point.

Here are three additional rules:

- ◆ Do not list any publication in your reference list that you do not cite.
- ◆ Do not cite any reference without placing it in the reference list.
- ◆ If you want to cite a source that you did not read, use the following format: "In Virgil's epic poem, The Aeneid, as cited by Allport and Postman (1947), the following characterization of rumor appears: . . ." But do this only if the original source is unavailable to you; otherwise examine and cite the original source yourself.

In general, there are two categories of citations in student research reports and essays (you will find many examples of each in the three sample papers). One category consists of citations that appear as part of the narrative; the other category consists of citations inserted in alphabetical order (and then by year if the same author is cited twice) entirely in parentheses within the narrative.

### Citation Appearing as Part of Narrative

```
Baldwin, Doyle, Kern, and Mithalal (1991) asked a sample of

child-care providers to describe incidents in which. . . .
```

## Citation Entirely in Parentheses

Institutional review boards may harbor quite different biases regarding the ethical risks of the studies they are asked to evaluate (e.g., Ceci, Peters, & Plotkin, 1985; Hamsher & Reznikoff, 1967; Kallgren & Kenrick, 1990; Schlenker & Forsyth, 1977).

These examples also illustrate the convention of author-date citations that dictates the listing of the surnames of up to five authors the first time the citation is given. In subsequent citations, if there are more than two authors, you mention the surname of only the first author followed by *et al.* and the date, for example:

### Subsequent Citation as Part of Narrative

Ceci et al. (1985) found that a proposal, approved without changes in one institution, was amended at another institution in the same city.

### Subsequent Citation Entirely in Parentheses

A research proposal, approved without changes in one institution, was amended at another institution in the same city (Ceci et al., 1985).

Notice that in the initial pair of citations on pages 77 and 78 the word *and* is spelled out in the narrative citation but that an ampersand (&) is used in the parenthetical citation. Here are some other specific rules that cover most simple cases:

◆ If you are citing a series of works, the proper sequence is by alphabetical order of the surname of the first author and then by chronological order (Crabb, 1990; DiFonzo & Bordia, 1993; Fung, 1989, 1990; Gergen & Shotter, 1985, 1988; Hilbert & Brecher, 1996; Stern, in press; Strohmetz, 1991; Trimble, in press; Wells & Lafleur, 1996).

◆ Two or more works published by the same author in the same year are designated as *a, b, c,* and so on (Hantula, 1996a, 1996b, 1996c). In the reference list, the alphabetical order of the works' titles determines the sequence when there is more than one work by the author in the same year.

◆ Work accepted for publication but not yet printed is designated "in press" (Hesson, in press); in a list of citations, the rule is to place this work last: (Hesson, 1993, 1996, in press).

What should you do if you run into a problem that these rules do not address? If your instructor is a stickler for the APA style of handling citations, then look in the most recent edition of the *Publication Manual of the American Psychological Association*. We are not sticklers and only recommend that you keep one general idea in mind as you go beyond these specific guidelines: *If you run into a problem, use common sense.* Ask yourself whether you could find the reference referred to based on the citation you have provided. In other words, put yourself in your reader's shoes.

## Tables and Figures

Tables and figures may be used to augment the presentation of the results. Often, when students include tables in their research reports, the instructor finds that they are merely presenting their raw data in a neat format. Save your raw data for the appendix of your report (if your raw data are required), as shown in Bruce's report. Keep in mind that statistical tables in research reports should contain *summaries* of the raw data rather than the actual data (see Table 1 of Bruce's report) and other results.

The APA publication manual requires that tables and figures be put on separate pages at the end of the paper. However, it is often convenient (and more accessible to readers) to insert the table or figure in the main body of the paper. In Bruce's report the table is set into a page of text; in Peter's report the figure is placed on a separate page within the main body of the text. If your instructor does not object, you may use any of these styles; the rule of thumb is that your discussion must be easy to follow. Notice that the title of Bruce's Table 1 is shown above the table, and all information in the table is double-spaced.

It is also possible to use a *figure*, which is any type of exhibit or illustration other than a table. An easy way to differentiate between tables and figures is to think of tables in journal articles as typeset but figures as photographed from artwork. Peter's Figure 1 is called a bar chart or histogram. Observe that the caption (the title of the figure) goes below the figure, and that it begins with an uppercase letter and ends with a period. If you are working with a graphics program, you can compose the figure on the computer. The basic rule is to use figures that add to the text; do not simply repeat what you can say very clearly in words in the text. Sometimes elaborate figures introduce distortions, thus detracting from a clear, concise summary of the data. Be sure not to overcomplicate your figure; try it out on a friend to see if he or she understands it. A useful reference is S. M. Kosslyn's *Elements of Graph Design* (W. H. Freeman, 1994), which examines the legibility of graphs and other displays from the perspective of what we know about human cognition.

However you choose to display your findings in the research report, the title or caption must be clearly and precisely stated. If you need to add some clarifying or explanatory note to your table, it is customary to place this information below the table in a note, for example:

Note. The possible range of scores was from 1 (strong dis-

agreement) to 5 (strong agreement), with 3 indicating no

opinion.

If you want to make specific notes, the convention is to use superscript lowercase letters ($^a$ $^b$ $^c$) or asterisks(* ** ***). The following cases illustrate this usage:

**Superscript Notation**

$$^a\underline{n} = 50 \quad ^b\underline{n} = 62$$

**Asterisk Notation**

$$*\underline{p} < .05 \quad **\underline{p} < .01 \quad ***\underline{p} < .005$$

The following guidelines will prove helpful if you are preparing a figure:

- ◆ The figure should be neat, clearly presented, and precisely labeled to augment your discussion.
- ◆ The figure should be large enough to read easily.
- ◆ The units should progress from small to large.
- ◆ The data should be precisely plotted. If you are drawing the figure by hand, use graph paper to help you keep the rows and columns evenly spaced.
- ◆ When graphing the relationship between an independent variable and a dependent variable (or between a predictor variable and a criterion variable), it is customary to put the independent (or predictor) variable on the horizontal axis and the dependent (or criterion) variable on the vertical axis.

# Reference List

The reference list starts on a new page. The order of references is arranged alphabetically by the surname of the author(s) and then by the date of publication. The standard style recommended in the APA manual is to:

- ◆ Invert all authors' names (that is, last name, first initial, middle initial).

◆ List authors' names in the exact order in which they appear on the title page of the publication.
◆ Use commas to separate authors and an ampersand (&) before the last author.
◆ Give the year the work was copyrighted (the year and month for magazine articles and the year, month, and day for newspaper articles).
◆ For titles of books, chapters in books, and journal articles, capitalize only the first word of the title and of the subtitle (if any) as well as any proper names.
◆ Give the issue number of the journal if the article cited is paginated by issue.
◆ Underline the volume number of a journal article and the title of a book or a journal.
◆ Give the city of a book's publisher.
◆ If the city is not well known or might be confused with another location (for instance, Cambridge, Massachusetts, and Cambridge, England), give the state (or country).
◆ When in doubt about whether to list the state, list it.
◆ Use the postal abbreviation; for instance, *MA* for "Massachusetts."

Using these pointers, the examples in the three sample papers, and the following examples as general guidelines, you should encounter few problems. If you do run into one, however, the rule of thumb is to be clear, consistent, and complete in listing your source material:

## Authored Book (One or More Authors)

Lana, R. E. (1991). <u>Assumptions of social psychology:</u> <u>A reexamination.</u> Hillsdale, NJ: Erlbaum.

Levin, J., & Arluke, A. (1987). <u>Gossip: The inside scoop.</u> New York: Plenum Press.

Webb, E. J., Campbell, D. T., Schwartz, R. D., & Sechrest, L. (1966). <u>Unobtrusive measures: Nonreactive</u> <u>research in the social sciences.</u> Chicago: Rand-McNally.

## Work in Press (Edited Volume, Journal Article, Authored Book)

Blanck, P. D. (Ed.). (in press). <u>Interpersonal expecta-</u> <u>tions: Theory, research, and applications.</u> New York: Cambridge University Press.

Fine, G. A. (in press). The city as a folklore generator: Urban legends in the metropolis. <u>Urban Resources</u>.

Kapferer, J. (in press). <u>Rumors: Uses, interpretations, and images.</u> New Brunswick, NJ: Transaction Publishers.

## Edited Published Work (One or More Editors)

Morawski, J. G. (Ed.). (1988). <u>The rise of experimentation in American psychology.</u> New Haven: Yale University Press.

Gergen, K. J., & Gergen, M. (Eds.). (1984). <u>Historical social psychology.</u> Hillsdale, NJ: Erlbaum.

## Work Republished at a Later Date
## (Single or Multivolume Book and Anthology)

Demosthenes. (1852). <u>The Olynthiac and other public orations of Demosthenes.</u> London: Henry G. Bohn. (Original work written 349 B.C.)

Lessing, G. E. (1779/1971). <u>Gotthold Ephraim Lessing: Werke</u> (Vol. 2). München, Germany: Carl Hanser Verlag.

Pope, A. (1733/1903). Moral essays: Epistle I. To Sir Richard Temple, Lord Cobham, of the knowledge and character of men. In H. W. Boynton (Ed.), <u>The complete poetical works of Pope</u> (pp. 157-160). Boston: Houghton Mifflin.

## Journal Article Paginated by Volume (One or More Authors)

Scott-Jones, D. (1994). Ethical issues in reporting and referring in research with low-income minority children. <u>Ethics and Behavior, 42,</u> 97-108.

Arms, R. L., Russell, G. W., & Sandilands, M. L. (1979). Effects on the hostility of spectators' viewing aggressive sports. <u>Social Psychology Quarterly, 42,</u> 275-279.

## Article Paginated by Issue (Newsletter and Journal)

Goldstein, J. H. (1978). In vivo veritas: Has humor research looked at humor? Humor Research Newsletter, 3(1), 3-4.

Valdiserri, R. O., Tama, G. M., & Ho, M. (1988). The role of community advisory committees in clinical trials of anti-HIV agents. IRB: A Review of Human Subjects Research, 10(4), 5-7.

## Article in Foreign Language

Foa, U. G. (1966). Le nombre huit dans la socialization de l'enfant [The number eight in the socialization of the infant]. Bulletin du Centre d'Études et Recherches Psychologiques, 15, 39-47.

## Chapter in Multivolume Edited Series
## (Same or Different Author and Editor)

Kipnis, D. (1984). The use of power in organizations and interpersonal settings. In S. Oskamp (Ed.), Applied social psychology (Vol. 5, pp. 171-210). Newbury Park, CA: Sage.

Koch, S. (1959). General introduction to the series. In S. Koch (Ed.), Psychology: A study of a science (Vol. 1 pp. 1-18). New York: McGraw-Hill.

## Mass Media Article (Magazine or Newspaper)

Rowan, R. (1979, August 13). Where did that rumor come from? Fortune, pp. 130-137.

Sexton, J. (1990, January 14). Rumors have effect on Rangers. The New York Times, Section 8, pp. 1, 4.

## Doctoral Dissertation Abstract

Esposito, J. (1987). Subjective factors and rumor transmission: A field investigation of the influence of anxiety, importance, and belief on rumormongering (Doctoral dissertation, Temple University, 1986). Dissertation Abstracts International, 48, 596B.

## Technical Report

Kipnis, D., & Kidder, L. H. (1977). Practice performance and sex: Sex role appropriateness, success and failure as determinants of men's and women's task learning capabilities (Report No. 1). Philadelphia: University City Science Center.

## Unpublished Manuscript

Kimmel, A. J., & Keefer, R. (1989). Psychological correlates of the acceptance and transmission of rumors about AIDS. Unpublished manuscript.

## Paper Presented at a Meeting

Lamberth, J. (1981, January). Jury selection: A psychological approach. Paper presented at the meeting of the American Trial Assocation, Moorestown, NJ.

## Poster Presented at a Meeting

Walker, C. J., & Blaine, B. E. (1989, April). The virulence of dread rumors: A field experiment. Poster presented at the meeting of the Eastern Psychological Association, Boston.

# Proofing and Correcting

We now come to the final steps before you submit your paper: proofing and correcting. Read the finished manuscript more than once. Ask yourself the following questions:

- ◆ Are there omissions?
- ◆ Are there misspellings?
- ◆ Are the numbers correct?
- ◆ Are the hyphenations correct?
- ◆ Are all the references cited in the body of the paper in the references section?

The first time you read your final draft, the appeal of the neat, clean copy can lead you to overlook errors. Put the paper aside for 24 hours, and then read it carefully again. If you find errors, correct them before you submit the finished product. If you typed the paper and find small mistakes, use correction fluid to cover them and make the required corrections (but do not just type over an incorrect letter or number). If you typed the paper and find a substantial omission or many such omissions, retype the entire page.

Give your paper a final look, checking to be sure all the pages are there and in order. If you adhered to the guidelines in this manual, you should have the sense of a job well done and should feel confident that the paper will receive the serious attention that a clear, consistent, and attractive manuscript deserves.

# APPENDIX A

# Sample Essay

Intelligence  1


The Multiplex vs. g-centric View of Intelligence:
With Particular Emphasis on Gardner's Theory


Anne A. Skleder


Term Paper
(Number and Name of Course)
Instructor: (Name)
(Date Submitted)

Intelligence  2

Abstract

Two views of intelligence are discussed, the g-centric and
the "multiplex" positions. The classic g-centric view pro-
ceeds on the assumption that there is a common element
(i.e., "g") in all measures of intelligence. The multiplex
view is that there are many kinds of intelligence, and
they do not necessarily have a common psychometric core.
Illustrative of this view is the work of Gardner, which is
discussed here. Along with the criticisms of this theory,
I also speculate on the direction of future work on intelligence.

Introduction

Two Views of Intelligence

We speak of "intelligence" all the time, in many different contexts. Sometimes we call people "book smart," implying that they are strong in verbal or mathematical skills. We also talk of people who can "read others like a book" or those who are "street smart" (i.e., astute in the ways of the world). We turn to these individuals for advice when we are uncertain about the motives of others. We also speak of some people as having "business savvy" or "political sense," by which we mean they are adept in specialized ways that may not be directly measured by IQ tests.

The purpose of this essay is to explain two different views of intelligence--the traditional "g-centric" view and the view of intelligence as pluralistic (e.g., Sternberg & Detterman, 1986). I will use the term multiplex to characterize the pluralistic view in order to convey the idea of many legitimate intelligences that are housed within the same culture but not necessarily in any single individual within the culture. In particular, I will examine a pluralistic theory that has been proposed by Howard Gardner. I will describe the basis of his theorizing and then discuss some criticisms that have been leveled against this theory.

The g-centric View

For much of this century, the research on intelligence has concentrated on the existence of a general overriding

factor of intelligence (called "g") which is usually measured by tests of mathematical and linguistic skills.
Influenced by the seminal work of Charles Spearman (1927),
researchers in the intelligence test movement have
accepted this g-centric (i.e., g-centered) approach, arguing that g (viz., the general overriding factor of intelligence) is measured by every task in an intelligence test
(Gardner, 1983, 1985).

Likewise, in the area of child development, the follow-
ers of Jean Piaget have argued for the existence of general structures of the mind (Siegler & Richards, 1982).
These structures develop in the same way in all children,
so this argument goes. In the biological realm, some
researchers have attempted to operationalize g by measuring the speed of neural transmission (Reed & Jensen, 1992)
or through measures of hemispheric localization (Levy,
1974). A recent reanalysis of IQ data by Herrnstein and
Murray (1994) ignited debate about the role of g in the
lives of individuals and in the larger social order.

For some time, it has also been assumed that standard
tests based on the g-centric theory of intelligence provide magical numbers that allow us to distinguish "bright"
people from the "not-so-bright" in terms of accrued knowledge or potential for learning. The criticism of this
approach argues that IQ should not be viewed as an entity
distinct from other "intellectual" skills. For example,
Sternberg and Berg (1986) observed that a panel of experts
emphasized the roles of context, metacognition, and culture in the attributes they associated with intelligence.

The Multiplex View

Not surprisingly, there is still considerable contro-
versy about the meaning of intelligence, although a recent
task force established by the American Psychological
Association was able to point out some "knowns" about
intelligence that appear to be generally accepted in psychology (Neisser et al., 1996). Nevertheless, Sternberg
(1990) has argued that the nature of information processing measured by traditional IQ tests is really quite different from that involved in certain complex reasoning in
everyday life. For example, Ceci and Liker (1986) reported
that skill in handicapping race horses cannot be predicted
from performance on the Wechsler Adult Intelligence Scale.

Sternberg's argument and Ceci and Liker's findings are
also indicative of the multiplex view of intelligence. In
contrast to the g-centric view of intelligence as relatively simple in structure, the multiplex view encompasses
the idea of "multiple" and "systems" approaches (e.g.,
Ceci, 1990; Gardner, 1983; Sternberg, 1985). The multiplex
view assumes the existence of intelligences beyond the
verbal or mathematical realm. In the remainder of this
paper I focus on one approach as illustrative of the multiplex viewpoint: the theory of multiple intelligences put
forward by Howard Gardner (1983, 1993). In the tradition
of L. L. Thurstone (1938), Gardner has argued against considering intelligence in the singular, or even viewing
intelligence as multidimensional. Instead, he uses the
plural intelligences to characterize a number of different
talents.

Gardner's Theory of "Intelligences"

Definition of Intelligence

Gardner (1983) conceives of intelligence as "the ability to solve problems, or to create products that are valued within one or more cultural settings" (p. x). In spite of this rather broad definition, he goes on to argue that not every skill should be considered as falling under the umbrella label of intelligence. Rather, he argues that a talent must fit the following eight criteria to be considered an "intelligence" (Gardner, 1983):

1. The potential must exist to isolate the intelligence by brain damage;

2. Exceptional populations, such as savants, whose members exhibit outstanding but uneven abilities, provide evidence for the distinctive existence of a particular entity;

3. An intelligence must contain core operations, that is, basic information-processing operations that are unique to the particular abilities;

4. Any intelligence must have a distinctive developmental history, or developmental stages through which individuals pass, with individual differences in the ultimate levels of expertise achieved;

5. We must be able to locate antecedents (more primitive, less integrated versions) of an intelligence in other species;

6. An intelligence must be open to experimental study, so that the predictions of the theory can be subjected to empirical tests;

7. Although no test can measure the entirety of abilities that are deemed intellectual, standardized tests provide clues about an intelligence when the items on the test predict the performance of some tasks and not others;

8. We must be able to capture the information content in an intelligence through a symbol system, such as language or choreographed movements.

Seven Kinds of Intelligence

Based on these requirements, Gardner argues the importance of studying people within the "normal" range of intelligence but also studying those who are gifted or expert in various domains valued by different cultures. He also emphasizes the importance of studying individuals who have suffered selective brain injuries. Using his eight criteria, and research results from psychology, sociology, anthropology, and biology, he proposed the existence of seven intelligences.

Traditional intelligence, which is language-based and easy to quantify by traditional measures, is located within the first two intelligences: logical-mathematical and linguistic intelligence. People who are high in logical and mathematical intelligence are identified as skilled in reasoning and computation. People with keen linguistic skills are good with words and language. However, Gardner believes these two kinds of intelligence represent only part of the picture. Thus he theorizes five additional kinds of intelligence: spatial, bodily-kinesthetic, musical, intrapersonal, and interpersonal.

Spatial intelligence is demonstrated by those who are
able to navigate the spatial world with ease.
Bodily-kinesthetic intelligence is the domain of dancers,
athletes, neurosurgeons, and others who are skilled in
carrying and moving their bodies. One who is musically
intelligent is talented in discerning themes in music and
is sensitive to qualities of music (e.g., pitch, rhythm,
and timbre). The last two intelligences are part of the
so-called personal intelligences, or the talent to detect
various shades of meaning in the emotions, intentions, and
behavior of ourselves (intrapersonal) or others (interpersonal). Those with intrapersonal expertise are adept at
self-understanding, while those who are high in interpersonal intelligence are "people persons" who always seem to
have a fix on the social landscape.

Independence of Abilities

Crucial to Gardner's formulation of multiple intelligences is that various "talents" are not necessarily
linked. Someone may perform very poorly in one area (e.g.,
logical-mathematical) and yet perform well in others
(e.g., spatial). This calls to mind the brilliant but
absent-minded professor, who cannot find the car in the
parking lot but can describe in intricate detail the inner
workings of automobiles. Different intelligences can
exist, and presumably be measured, quite independently of
one another, according to Gardner's theory. However, he
argues, because logical-mathematical and linguistic intelligences are valued in American schools, tests aiming to

measure a variety of intelligences still rely heavily on
mathematical and verbal skills.

In other words, conventional tests of intelligence measure the same intelligences in slightly different, and
perhaps trivial, ways. Therefore, it is not surprising
that factor analytic research (e.g., Spearman, 1927) has
often demonstrated a correlation among certain abilities
(implying the g factor), so that individuals who score
higher in verbal intelligence tend to score higher than
average in reasoning ability. However, knowing someone's
linguistic intelligence does not necessarily tell us very
much about the person's skills with people, music, or in
any other intellectual realm.

The independence of abilities is also suggested by the
fact that while intelligence tests predict school grades
reasonably well, they are far less useful in predicting
routine successes outside the school setting. Barring low
levels of traditional IQ, the strength of a manager, for
example, may be related to a far greater extent to the
ability to manage oneself and the task completion of
others than to the ability to score high on an IQ test
(Sternberg, 1988). Sternberg (1988, p. 211) calls this
skill "practical intelligence" (and distinguishes it from
academic intelligence), which in this case seems to be
heavily dependent on what Gardner called the personal
intelligences.

### Criticisms of Multiplex Theories

#### Nontraditional Orientation

Most criticisms of multiplex theories seem to rest on
the distinction between intelligence and abilities that

Intelligence 10

have been traditionally characterized as talents (Walters & Gardner, 1986). Interestingly, Sternberg (1990), one of the pioneers in the development of multiplex theories of intelligence, mentions that an individual who has experienced an injury that causes a loss of bodily-kinesthetic ability is not viewed as "mentally retarded." By the same token, we might ask why a person very low in social skills, but who scores in the range of normal on IQ tests, is not regarded as "mentally retarded."

Gardner answers that this criticism is simply burdened by a traditional definition of intelligence that he does not use in his theory. Rather, he argues that bodily-kinesthetic (as well as all of the other forms of intelligence he proposes) should be given equal consideration with the logical-mathematical and linguistic forms of intelligence so highly valued in Western cultures (Walters & Gardner, 1986). Perhaps it is only because we have chosen to consider the "academic" intelligences as more important than the interpersonal type, that the term socially retarded is not in common usage. Interestingly, renewed interest in the social origins of intelligence is leading to increased attention to the interplay of interpersonal skills and success (e.g., Rosnow, Skleder, Jaeger, & Rind, 1994).

Structure and Amenability to Tests

A second criticism is that, given the amorphous structure of multiplex theories, there are unlimited possibilities to increase the number of intelligences beyond even the seven forms proposed by Gardner. Since the initial presentation of his theory, he has suggested the possibility of _more_ than seven intelligences and considers the seven intelligences to be "working hypotheses" fully amenable to revision after further investigation (Walters & Gardner, 1986). Whether this criticism is reasonable or not seems to rest on whether one is willing to consider intelligence as even more inclusive of human talents than it is being viewed currently.

It has also been argued that more conventional theories, such as the psychometric approach, have the advantage of being more amenable to testing and measurement than is the theory of multiple intelligences. However, Gardner contends that his intelligences are measurable, but that conventional paper-and-pencil tests are inadequate for the job. Instead, he suggests measurements that are more closely linked to what people do in their daily lives--inside and outside of academic settings. For example, in applying his theory to education, Gardner (1991, 1993) has reported assessing children's intelligences by studying their school compositions, choice of activities, performance in athletic events, and other aspects of their behavior and cognitive processes. While this is certainly more difficult and complex, these types of measurements are necessary from the standpoint of Gardner's theory.

### Conclusions

Clearly, the challenge remains to develop new ways (however complex and nontraditional) to measure the dif-

ferent facets of intelligence (Neisser et al., 1996). In
particular, I focused on one theory representing the multiplex approach, Gardner's theory of multiple intelligences. This theory encompasses the aspects of traditional
intelligence but also attempts to move our conceptualiza-
tion of intelligence beyond the traditional boundaries.
For example, when Gardner (1983) considers a great dancer
to be "kinesthetically intelligent," he is talking about a
skill that Spearman would not have considered to belong
within the category of intelligence. That Gardner's model
is so much broader than the traditional model of intelligence is viewed from some perspectives to be a problem,
because the broader the theory, the more difficult it is
to disconfirm. However, based on my literature search I
discerned a trend toward broad, interdisciplinary formula-
tions rather than more narrow ways of conceptualizing
intelligence. With this broader approach, many researchers
are now including a focus on skills that in the past were
either ignored or considered to be far less important than
academic intelligence.

Intelligence 13

References

Ceci, S. J. (1990). <u>On intelligence...more or less: A</u>
<u>bioecological treatise on intellectual development.</u>
Englewood Cliffs, NJ: Prentice Hall.

Ceci, S. J., & Liker, J. (1986). Academic and nonacade-
mic intelligence: An experimental separation. In R. J.
Sternberg & R. Wagner (Eds.), <u>Practical intelligence:</u>
<u>Origins of competence in the everyday world</u> (pp 119-142).
New York: Cambridge University Press.

Gardner, H. (1983). <u>Frames of mind: The theory of mul-</u>
<u>tiple intelligences.</u> New York: Basic Books.

Gardner, H. (1985). <u>The mind's new science.</u> New York:
Basic Books.

Gardner, H. (1991). Assessment in context: The alterna-
tive to standardized testing. In B. R. Gifford & M. C.
O'Connor (Eds.), <u>Changing assessments: Alternative views</u>
<u>of aptitude, achievement and instruction</u> (pp. 77-119).
Boston: Kluwer.

Gardner, H. (1993). <u>Multiple intelligences: The theory</u>
<u>in practice.</u> New York: Basic Books.

Herrnstein, R. J., & Murray, C. (1994). <u>The bell curve:</u>
<u>Intelligence and class structure in American life.</u> New
York: Free Press.

Levy, J. (1974). Cerebral asymmetries as manifested in
split-brain man. In M. Kinsbourne & W. L. Smith (Eds.),
<u>Hemispheric disconnection and cerebral function</u> (pp.
165-183). Springfield, IL: Charles C Thomas.

Neisser, U., Boodoo, G., Bouchard, T. J., Jr., Boykin,
A. W., Brody, N., Ceci, S. J., Halpern, D. F., Loehlin,
J. C., Perloff, R., Sternberg, R. J., & Urbina, S. (1996).

Intelligence  14

Intelligence: Knowns and unknowns. American Psychologist,
51, 77-101.

Reed, T. E., & Jensen, A. R. (1992). Conduction veloc-
ity in a brain nerve pathway of normal adult correlates
with intelligence. Intelligence, 16, 259-272.

Rosnow, R. L., Skleder, A. A., Jaeger, M. E., & Rind,
B. (1994). Intelligence and the epistemics of interpersonal acumen: Testing some implications of Gardner's theory. Intelligence, 19, 93-116.

Siegler, R. S., & Richards, D. D. (1982). The development of intelligence. In R. J. Sternberg (Ed.), Handbook
of human intelligence (pp. 897-971). New York: Cambridge
University Press.

Spearman, C. (1927). The abilities of man. New York:
Macmillan.

Sternberg, R. J. (1985). Beyond IQ: A triarchic theory
of human intelligence. New York: Cambridge University
Press.

Sternberg, R. J. (1988). The triarchic mind: A new theory of human intelligence. New York: Viking.

Sternberg, R. J. (1990). Metaphors of mind: Conceptions
of the nature of intelligence. New York: Cambridge
University Press.

Sternberg, R. J., & Berg, C. A. (1986). Definitions of
intelligence: A comparison of the 1921 and 1986 symposia.
In R. J. Sternberg & D. K. Detterman (Eds.), What is
intelligence? Contemporary viewpoints on its nature and
definition (pp. 155-162). Norwood, NJ: Ablex.

Intelligence   15

Sternberg, R. J., & Detterman, D. K. (Eds.). (1986).
What is intelligence? Contemporary viewpoints on its
nature and definition. Norwood, NJ: Ablex.

Thurstone, L. L. (1938). Primary mental abilities.
Chicago: University of Chicago Press.

Walters, J. M., & Gardner, H. (1986). The theory of
multiple intelligences: Some issues and answers. In R. J.
Sternberg and R. K. Wagner (Eds.), Practical intelligence:
Nature and origins of competence in the everyday world
(pp. 163-182). New York: Cambridge University Press.

# APPENDIX B

# Sample Experimental Research Report

Tipping Behavior  1

Effect of an After-Meal Mint on Restaurant Tipping:
An Experimental Study in a Naturalistic Setting

Bruce Rind

Research Report
(Number and Name of Course)
Instructor: (Name)
(Date Submitted)

Abstract

Previous research has shown that servers can increase
their tips by using a variety of techniques that generally
involve creating an impression of friendliness. I examined
another technique that was expected to increase customers'
favorable impressions of servers, and hence tip percentages as well. Servers either did or did not give customers
a small gift (individually wrapped mints) with the check.
When presenting the gift, sometimes servers took credit
for it and sometimes they attributed it to the restaurant;
the purpose of this manipulation was to examine whether a
reciprocity effect might result. No reciprocity effect
resulted, but there was a large effect for presentation of
the gift. Servers averaged 19% tips when not presenting
the gift, and 28% when the gift was presented.

Introduction

More than one million people in the United States work
as waiters or waitresses (Department of Commerce, 1990, p.
391). Although these servers are generally paid for their
service by their employers, the major source of income for
servers usually comes in the form of tips from customers
(Lynn & Mynier, 1993; Schmidt, 1985). Because tips are so
important to the livelihood of most servers, knowledge
about factors that affect customers' tipping behavior is
valuable. Over the last decade, a growing number of studies have examined factors hypothesized to affect tipping.
This research has shown that servers can increase their
tipping percentages by a variety of techniques (Lynn,
1996).

Some of these techniques involve direct interpersonal
action on the part of the server, such as touching or
smiling at the customer. Hornik (1992) had three waitresses at two restaurants either not touch their customers, touch them for half a second on the shoulder, or
touch them twice on the palm of the hand for half a second
each time. Tips increased from 12% to 14% to 17% in the
three conditions, respectively. Tidd and Lockard (1978)
had a waitress give customers sitting alone a large,
open-mouth smile or a small, closed-mouth smile. Customers
in the former condition tipped on average 48 cents compared to 20 cents in the latter condition. In a similar
vein, Lynn and Mynier (1993) instructed servers either to
squat to the eye level of their customers or stand erect
during the initial visit to the table, with the result

that squatting increased tips. Garrity and Degelman (1990) reported that a server earned higher tips when she introduced herself to her customers by her first name during her initial visit (23% average tip) than when she did not introduce herself (15% average tip).

Other effective techniques employed an indirect stimulus to stimulate tipping. Rind and Bordia (1996) had servers either draw or not draw a happy face on the back of customer checks before delivering them. The happy face increased tips for the female server, but did not increase tips for the male server (for whom this practice may have been viewed as gender-inappropriate by customers). Rind and Bordia (1995) also found that having "thank you" on the back of customer checks resulted in an increase from 16% to 18%. Finally, McCall and Belmont (1995) had servers present checks either on a tray with credit card emblems on it or on a tray with no emblems and found that tip percentages were higher in the former condition.

These techniques, except for the last one, have in common that the servers are doing something that is likely to increase the customers' impressions of friendliness. In the present study, another such technique was experimentally examined. When servers at a restaurant-diner delivered checks to customers, they sometimes also delivered an accompanying gift (a moderately priced mint). This gift, it was hypothesized, would be viewed by customers as a gesture of friendliness, which would have the effect of increasing tips. When delivering the mint, sometimes servers said it came from them, and other times they told the customers that the mint was from the restaurant. It was also hypothesized that customers who were told the gift came from the server would tip more than customers who were told the gift came from the restaurant. This expectation follows from research on reciprocity (Regan, 1971), in which individuals feel especially obligated to return a favor to the person responsible for the favor (e.g., a server who gives his or her own gift rather than a gift from the restaurant).

Method

Subjects

Seventy-five parties who were having lunch at a suburban Philadelphia restaurant-diner served as subjects. The dining parties consisted of a total of 213 customers, with a mean of 2.8 customers per party ($\underline{SD}$ = 0.6).

Procedure

The experiment was conducted over a 4-day period from Monday through Thursday during June 1996. Three female servers and one male server, ranging in age from 32 to 53, acted as the experimental accomplices. Two female servers worked the afternoon shift from noon until 6 p.m. The third female server and the male server worked the evening shift from 5 p.m. until 11 p.m.

A stack of 75 index cards was shuffled and placed in a bag in the kitchen. These cards were used to determine the experimental condition for each dining party. Twenty-five cards had written on them "no mints," constituting the control condition. A second group of 25 cards had written on them "mints" along with the phrase "here are some mints

from the restaurant," constituting the low-reciprocity
mint condition. A third group of 25 cards also had written
on them "mints," but this word was followed by the phrase
"here are some mints from me," constituting the high-reciprocity mint condition.

At the end of dining parties' meals, when it was time
for servers to present the check, the servers went into
the kitchen, reached into a bag, and drew one of the cards
in the bag. In this fashion, random assignment of subjects
to conditions (with an equal number of dining parties per
condition) was achieved. If a "no mint" card was drawn,
servers presented the check without a mint. If "mint"
appeared, servers presented mints (creme de menthe thins
in green foil), one mint per customer in the party.
Additionally, servers repeated the phrase depending on the
card they had drawn. To avoid possible confounding of
extraneous variables with experimental conditions, servers
were instructed to behave consistently when presenting the
check and to avoid extraneous interactions with the party
after presenting the check.

When dining parties left the table, servers recorded on
the same index card used to determine the experimental
condition the amount of the bill before taxes, the tip
amount, and the number of customers in the party. The
dependent measure was defined as the tip percentage, which
was calculated by dividing the amount of the tip by the
size of the bill before taxes and multiplying this value
by 100.

Table 1

Mean Tip Percentages and Standard Deviations as a Function of Serving After-Meal Mints and Attributing This Gift to the Restaurant or to the Server

| | | Mints from | |
| Results | No mint | Restaurant | Server |
|---------|---------|------------|--------|
| M | 18.94 | 27.99 | 27.82 |
| SD | 4.95 | 10.62 | 8.96 |

Results

Table 1 shows the tip percentage (i.e., the arithmetic mean, M, of the percentages) and the standard deviation (SD) in each group (n = 25 per group). It was predicted that tip percentages would be higher when mints were given in the high-reciprocity mode ("mints from me") than in the low-reciprocity mode ("mints from restaurant"). Contrary to this prediction, the high-reciprocity condition did not result in a higher tip percentage (M = 27.82) than the low-reciprocity condition (M = 27.99), with $t(72)$ = .07 very close to the expected value of this statistic when the null hypothesis is true (i.e., $t$ = 0). It was further predicted that a gift of mints would increase tip percentages over no gift. To address this hypothesis, the mean percentage of the no-mint group was contrasted with the mean percentages of the two mint groups using contrast weights of -2, 1, and 1, respectively. This test was highly significant, $t(72)$ = 4.30, $p$ < .0001 one-tailed, and the effect size ($r$ = .45) was large, implying that serving mints increased tip percentages.

## Discussion

The results suggest that adding a small gift in the form of individually wrapped mints can improve servers' tip percentages. This finding adds to a growing list of techniques that servers can use to increase their income. Presenting the mints may have increased tips in this experiment because this practice may have conveyed a sense of friendliness to customers, who were then inclined to be helpful in return by tipping more (cf. Lynn & Mynier, 1993). If creating a perception of friendliness was the mechanism, then this technique is similar to many of the techniques reviewed by Lynn (1996) in terms of the process by which increased tips are elicited. Further research, however, is needed to establish this mechanism.

In this experiment the mean check for dining parties was $25.58. On average, presenting a check without mints yielded a tip of $4.84. By including mints, the tips increased on average to $7.14, which represents a mean increase of $2.30 per dining party. From this large increase, the small cost of mints should be deducted to assess the net gain. At 10 cents per mint, the average deduction would be 28 cents per dining party because the typical party consisted of 2.8 customers, yielding an average increase of $2.02. This 42% net increase represents a substantial gain in income for the servers, who depend largely on tips as their source of income. Thus, the finding that adding a small gift of relatively low cost had such a dramatic effect is important for servers.

Tipping Behavior   9

Contrary to expectations, higher reciprocity had no effect on tip percentages. Whether servers indicated the gift was from themselves or from the restaurant, customers tipped at the same rate. This finding contradicts previous research that reported that individuals feel especially inclined to return a favor to the sources responsible for the favor (Regan, 1971). This contradiction suggests that further research should be conducted to examine the replicability of the present finding. This study was conducted in a midscale restaurant-diner, and therefore it is also necessary to vary location and restaurant-type factors in future research to examine the generalizability of the data.

                                     Tipping Behavior   10
                            References
    Department of Commerce. (1990). Statistical abstracts
of the United States. Washington, DC: Author.

    Garrity, K., & Degelman, D. (1990). Effect of server
introduction on restaurant tipping. Journal of Applied
Social Psychology, 20, 168-172.

    Hornik, J. (1992). Tactile stimulation and consumer
response. Journal of Consumer Research, 19, 449-458.

    Lynn, M. (1996). Seven ways to increase servers' tips.
Cornell Hotel and Restaurant Administration Quarterly,
37(3), 24-29.

    Lynn, M., & Mynier, K. (1993). Effect of server posture
on restaurant tipping. Journal of Applied Social
Psychology, 23, 678-685.

    McCall, M., & Belmont, H. J. (1995). Credit card
insignia and tipping: Evidence for an associative link.
Unpublished manuscript, Ithaca College.

    Regan, D. T. (1971). Effects of a favor and liking on
compliance. Journal of Experimental Social Psychology, 7,
627-639.

    Rind, B., & Bordia, P. (1995). Effect of server's
"thank you" and personalization on restaurant
tipping. Journal of Applied Social Psychology, 25,
745-751.

    Rind, B., & Bordia, P. (1996). Effect of restaurant
tipping of male and female servers drawing a happy, smiling face on the backs of customers' checks. Journal of
Applied Social Psychology, 26, 218-225.

Tipping Behavior   11

    Schmidt, D. G. (1985). Tips: The mainstay of many hotel
workers' pay. <u>Monthly Labor Review, 108,</u> 50-61.

    Tidd, K., & Lockard, J. (1978). Monetary significance
of the affiliative smile: A case for reciprocal altruism.
<u>Bulletin of the Psychonomic Society, 11,</u> 344-346.

## Appendix

| No Mint | Mints from Restaurant | Mints from Server |
|---|---|---|
| 21.43 | 24.54 | 13.00 |
| 17.43 | 18.95 | 19.67 |
| 13.12 | 63.56 | 35.69 |
| 26.80 | 24.51 | 16.79 |
| 13.33 | 33.94 | 23.81 |
| 11.75 | 31.83 | 35.43 |
| 28.13 | 27.67 | 38.07 |
| 18.78 | 17.06 | 23.47 |
| 13.16 | 39.31 | 37.21 |
| 11.07 | 24.91 | 29.31 |
| 19.32 | 33.88 | 20.91 |
| 14.22 | 27.10 | 18.91 |
| 19.05 | 18.43 | 15.19 |
| 23.01 | 18.53 | 17.37 |
| 16.60 | 23.56 | 29.56 |
| 20.80 | 46.51 | 39.13 |
| 14.57 | 20.02 | 39.31 |
| 26.74 | 14.49 | 25.48 |
| 26.34 | 20.80 | 40.65 |
| 22.08 | 27.24 | 21.15 |
| 24.64 | 36.90 | 23.06 |
| 23.26 | 23.57 | 35.64 |
| 13.84 | 33.20 | 31.94 |
| 21.81 | 23.59 | 41.04 |
| 18.12 | 25.73 | 23.60 |

$$\overline{X} = \quad 18.94 \qquad\qquad 27.99 \qquad\qquad 27.82$$

$$S = \quad 4.95 \qquad\qquad 10.62 \qquad\qquad 8.96$$

$MSW = 72.47$

$df_w = 72$

$$t_{server\ vs.\ restaurant} = \frac{27.82 - 27.99}{\sqrt{72.47 \left(\frac{1}{25} + \frac{1}{25}\right)}} = -.07$$

$$t_{mints\ vs.\ no\ mint} = \frac{27.99 + 27.82 - 2(18.94)}{\sqrt{72.47 \left(\frac{1}{25} + \frac{1}{25} + \frac{4}{25}\right)}} = 4.30 \qquad r = \sqrt{\frac{4.3^2}{4.3^2 + 72}} = .45$$

# Sample Archival
# Research Report

Gender and Work   1


The Representation of Gender and Work in Children's Books:
An Archival Study Using Content Analysis



Peter B. Crabb



Research Report
(Number and Name of Course)
Instructor: (Name)
(Date Submitted)

Gender and Work    2

Abstract

This archival investigation used the method of content
analysis to reveal how work and gender were portrayed in
300 pictures in 130 award-winning children's books that
were published between 1937 and 1989. Two raters who independently coded the pictures were in substantial agreement
about the type of work activity portrayed. Female characters were more often shown as working in the household,
and male characters were more often shown as working outside the home. The discussion, which followed the lead of
Bussey and Perry (1982), argued that children's exposure
to such representations could result in expectations,
interests, and competencies that direct girls and boys to
model themselves after work roles defined by a traditional
gender-based division of labor.

Introduction

One of the main factors defining the division of labor
in industrialized societies is gender. Since the 18th century, women have typically been housekeepers and
child-caretakers and men have been wage-earners working
outside the home (Parsons, 1955). In the United States and
elsewhere, this division of labor has changed, however.
Over the last three decades, the proportion of single and
married women working outside the home in the United
States has increased dramatically (Department of Labor,
1991).

Despite this trend, there is evidence that children
continue to view work in and outside of the home as
gender-appropriate (Gettys & Cann, 1981). This finding
raises the possibility that children are being exposed to
stereotypical representations that link women to household
work and men to production outside the home. One plausible
source of such representations of gender and work may be
children's books.

To examine how high-profile books for children portray
work and gender, the method of content analysis was chosen. It was possible to categorize the qualitative data by
having raters tabulate the frequencies of occurrence of
sampling units (also called recording units and units of
analysis) of theoretical interest (Elder, Pavalko, &
Clipp, 1993; Krippendorff, 1980). The following hypotheses
were tested:

Hypothesis 1. In comparison with male characters, a
larger proportion of female characters would be shown
doing household work in depictions of gender and work.

Gender and Work  4

Hypothesis 2. In comparison with female characters, a
larger proportion of male characters would be shown doing
production work outside the home.

Method

Unitizing Procedure

Krippendorff (1980) used the term "unitizing" (p. 57)
to refer to the process of defining and selecting the
recording or sampling units to be used in a content analysis. The unit of analysis in this study was defined as
illustrations of gender and work found in award-winning
children's books published in the United States between
1937 and 1989. Specifically, the sample of books chosen
was identified as having received the Newbery or Caldecott
Award (Association for Library Service to Children, 1990).
Presumably, such books would have had a high profile in
libraries and bookstores and were therefore assumed to
be representative of the reading material of American
children.

Only illustrations showing a character easily identified as male or female using a tool to perform some type
of work were used in this analysis. I identified 1,613
such illustrations, which, under the guidance of the
instructor, I pared down by the method of proportionate
sampling described by Kish (1965). This procedure uses
random sampling to identify representative proportions of
specified categories of events (e.g., male characters and
female characters using a tool to perform work). The original sample was reduced to 300 relevant illustrations, of
which 78 represented female characters and 222 represented

male characters. This sample included pictures from 130 of
the 220 books and represented every publication year from
1937 to 1989.

Raters and Recording

   Recording refers to the coding of data, in which raters
record the frequencies of occurrence of specific events or
variables of theoretical interest (Krippendorff, 1980). The
raters in this study were two female students enrolled in
an introductory psychology course who volunteered to participate. They were instructed to use the coding sheet
shown in Appendix A. For each book, the rater noted the
author's (illustrator's) name, a designated code number,
the year the book was published, its title, place of publication, publisher, and the total number of pages.

   In coding the illustrations, the rater noted the page
number of the illustration, the tool shown in the picture,
the type of work represented (household, production, or
other), and whether the person doing work was a child, an
adult, or unidentifiable as either, and also noted whether
that person was male, female, or unidentifiable by gender.
Household work was defined as "the use of tools in and
around the home to prepare food, to clean, and to care for
family members"; production work as "the use of tools outside the home for construction, agriculture, and transportation"; and other work as "work that did not qualify
as either household or production, including the use of
tools for leisure activities and for protection from the
elements."

Results

The interrater reliability for coding the type of work
was calculated by means of Cohen's kappa as described by
Fleiss (1981); all calculations are shown in Appendix B.
The higher the value of kappa, the more the agreement
indicated in the ratings of the two judges. These judges
independently coded the type of work into three categories, with the resulting kappa = .77. Using a general
rule of thumb noted by Elder et al. (1993, p. 43), this
magnitude of kappa implied "substantial agreement" between
the two judges.

Figure 1 (see next page) shows the results addressing
the two hypotheses in this study. Consistent with the
first hypothesis, there was a larger proportion of female
characters than male characters portrayed as engaging in
household work in the 55 illustrations of household work.
When I used a statistical procedure described by Fleiss
(1981), the difference between the two proportions was
found to be statistically significant with a large magnitude of effect ($Z$ = 5.68, $p$ < .000001 one-tailed, effect
size $r$ = .77). Consistent with the second hypothesis,
there was also a larger proportion of male characters than
female characters engaged in production work outside the
home in the 114 illustrations of production work ($Z$ =
5.88, $p$ < .0000001 one-tailed, effect size $r$ = .55).

Although not hypothesized, it was also of interest to
find out whether the proportions of female and male characters doing work not related to household or production
operations differed. A one-tailed $p$ level is appropriate

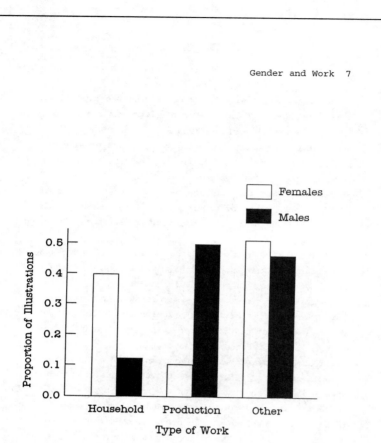

Figure 1. Proportions of illustrations (N = 300) as a function of gender and work.

Gender and Work   8

if a directional prediction was made, but a two-tailed p
was required in this case because this was an ad hoc prediction. For 131 illustrations showing other types of
work, the effect was small ($r$ = .11) and was not statistically significant ($Z$ = 1.31, p > .20 two-tailed).

Discussion

This study addressed the question of whether the culturally supplied representations of gender and work in
children's books reflected a stereotypical division of
labor. As hypothesized, female characters tended to be
shown working in the home while male characters tended to
be shown working outside the home. Work that is typically
unrelated to either household operations or production
activities was not portrayed as predominantly female or
male. Thus this particular sample of children's books
appears only to reflect traditional work roles for females
and males.

The findings are theoretically informative because of
their modeling implications. Modeling refers to the social
phenomenon in which someone who observes someone else (a
model) demonstrate certain behavior then copies the behavior. Such a phenomenon is apparently present in a range of
situations involving adults who copy the behavior of others (Rosenthal, 1966), and thus it seems plausible that
children should be susceptible to the effect of
gender-linked modeling (Bussey & Perry, 1982). That is to
say, children who observe the work behavior of characters
in books may as a consequence become more interested in
tools and skills modeled as appropriate for their own
gender.

Gender and Work  9

One limitation of this study is that only a small sample of award-winning books was examined. It may be that other books, television, and other media more accurately reflect different trends in work roles that are current in our culture. A second limitation is that I did not explore possible differences in the portrayal of work roles over time. Future research is needed to address these further issues and to examine the ways in which pictorial representations can affect children's expectations, attitudes, and behavior.

Gender and Work   10

References

Association for Library Service to Children. (1990).
The Newbery and Caldecott awards. Chicago: American
Library Association.

Bussey, K., & Perry, D. G. (1982). Same-sex imitation:
The avoidance of cross-sex models or the acceptance of
same-sex models? Sex Roles, 8, 773-784.

Department of Labor. (1991). Working women: A chartbook
(Bulletin 2385). Washington, DC: Bureau of Labor
Statistics.

Elder, G. H., Jr., Pavalko, E. K., & Clipp, E. C.
(1993). Working with archival data: Studying lives.
Newbury Park, CA: Sage.

Fleiss, J. L. (1981). Statistical methods for rates and
proportions. New York: Wiley.

Gettys, L. D., & Cann, A. (1981). Children's percep-
tions of occupational sex stereotypes. Sex Roles, 8,
301-308.

Kish, L. (1965). Survey sampling. New York: Wiley.

Krippendorff, K. (1980). Content analysis: An introduction to methodology. Newbury Park, CA: Sage.

Parsons, T. (1955). The American family: Its relation
to personality and social structure. In T. Parsons & R. F.
Bales (Eds.), Family, socialization and interaction
process (pp. 3-33). Glencoe, IL: Free Press.

Rosenthal, R. (1966). Experimenter effects in behavioral research. New York: Appleton-Century-Crofts.

Gender and Work   11

Appendix A
Coding Sheet Used by Raters

Author's, Illustrator's Name(s)     Book #

Pub. Date        Title

Place of Publication        Publisher

# Pages

| p.# | Tool Used | Work Type | | | Character | | | | | |
|-----|-----------|-----------|---|---|-----------|---|---|---|---|---|
| | | Hshold | Prdctn | Other | Age | | | Gender | | |
| | | | | | Ch | Ad | ? | F | M | ? |
| | | | | | | | | | | |
| | | | | | | | | | | |
| | | | | | | | | | | |
| | | | | | | | | | | |
| | | | | | | | | | | |
| | | | | | | | | | | |
| | | | | | | | | | | |
| | | | | | | | | | | |
| | | | | | | | | | | |
| | | | | | | | | | | |
| | | | | | | | | | | |
| | | | | | | | | | | |
| | | | | | | | | | | |
| | | | | | | | | | | |
| | | | | | | | | | | |

Gender and Work  13

Appendix B

Calculations on the Raw Data

<u>Interjudge Agreement</u>                    P. 1

$\underline{N} = 300$  illustrations

$\underline{n} = 2$  judges

$K = 3$  categories

$\underline{N_n} = 600$

(1)  $\sum_{n_j \text{ household}} = 7+17+13+21+12+10+5+24+4+17+7 = \quad 137$

$\sum_{nj \text{ Production}} = 19+40+21+22+17+22+2+26+6+16+8 = \quad 199$

$\sum_{nj \text{ other}} = 16+19+32+33+31+42+1+24+14+91+12 = \quad 265$

(2)  $\sum n^2_{nj \text{ Household}} = 13+27+25+35+20+18+9+46+8+25+11 = 237$

$\sum n^2_{nj \text{ production}} = 35+76+41+40+31+44+2+50+12+28+14 = 373$

$\sum n^2_{nj \text{ other}} = 30+37+64+59+59+82+1+46+28+73+23 = 502$

(3)  $P_{0 \text{ Household}} = \dfrac{137}{600} = .2293$

$P_{0 \text{ production}} = \dfrac{199}{600} = .3317$

$P_{0 \text{ other}} = \dfrac{265}{600} = .4417$

(4)  $\overline{P_0} = \dfrac{1}{N_n(n-1)} \left( \sum_{i=1}^{N} \sum_{j=1}^{n} n^2_{ij} - N_n \right)$

$= \dfrac{1}{(300)(2)(2-1)} \left( (502 + 237 + 373) - 300(2) \right)$

$= \dfrac{1}{600} \left( 1112 - 600 \right)$

$= .8533$

<u>Inter judge Agreement (cont.)</u>                    p. 2

⑤ $\overline{P_e} = \sum\limits_{j=1}^{k} P_j^2$

$= (.4417)^2 + (.2283)^2 + (.3317)^2$

$= .3572$

⑥ $Kappa = \dfrac{\overline{P_o} - \overline{P_e}}{1 - \overline{P_e}}$

$= \dfrac{.8533 - .3572}{1 - .3572}$

$= \boxed{+0.77}$

p.3

<u>Hypothesis 1 : $P_F > P_m$ (Household Work)</u>

<u>Total Sample</u>: $N = 300$, with $\underline{N}_F = 78$ and $\underline{N}_M = 222$

<u>Illustrations of Household Work</u>: $N = 55$, with $\underline{n}_F = 31$, $\underline{n}_m = 24$

$$\boxed{\text{Note}: \quad P = \text{"big } P\text{"}, \quad p = \text{"little } p\text{"}}$$

① $se_{P_F - P_m} = \sqrt{p\,(1-p)\left(\frac{1}{N_F} + \frac{1}{N_m}\right)}$ , where $p = \dfrac{n_F + n_m}{\underline{N}_F + \underline{N}_M}$

$$= \sqrt{.1833\,(.8167)\left(\frac{1}{78} + \frac{1}{222}\right)} \qquad = \frac{31 + 24}{78 + 222}$$

$$= .0509 \qquad\qquad\qquad\qquad\qquad\qquad = .1833$$

② $Z = \dfrac{P_F - P_m}{se_{P_F - P_m}}$ , where $P_F = \dfrac{n_F}{\underline{N}_F} = \dfrac{31}{78} = .3974$

$$= \frac{.3974 - .1081}{.0509} \qquad \text{and } P_M = \frac{n_m}{\underline{N}_M} = \frac{24}{222} = .1081$$

$$= \boxed{5.68}$$

③ Effect Size $\varnothing = \dfrac{Z}{\sqrt{N}}$

$$= \frac{5.68}{\sqrt{55}}$$

$$= \boxed{+0.77}$$

<u>Hypothesis 2 : $P_F < P_m$ (Production Work)</u>   P-4

<u>Total Sample:</u> $\underline{N} = 300$, with $\underline{N}_F = 78$ and $\underline{N}_m = 222$

<u>Illustrations of Production work:</u> $\underline{N} = 114$, with $\underline{n}_F = 8$ and $\underline{n}_m = 106$

$\boxed{\underline{Note}: P = \text{"big P"}, \quad p = \text{"little p"}}$

① $se_{P_m - P_F} = \sqrt{p(1-p)\left(\frac{1}{\underline{N}_F} + \frac{1}{\underline{N}_m}\right)}$ , where

$\qquad = \sqrt{.38\,(.62)\left(\frac{1}{78} + \frac{1}{222}\right)}$

$\qquad = .0638$

$p = \dfrac{n_F + n_m}{\underline{N}_F + \underline{N}_m}$

$\qquad = \dfrac{8 + 106}{78 + 222}$

$\qquad = .38$

② $Z = \dfrac{P_m - P_F}{se_{P_m - P_F}}$ , where $P_m = \dfrac{106}{222} = .478$

$\qquad\qquad\qquad\qquad\qquad P_F = \dfrac{8}{78} = .1026$

$\qquad = \dfrac{.478 - .1026}{.0638}$

$\qquad = \boxed{5.88}$

③ Effect Size $\phi = \dfrac{Z}{\sqrt{N}}$

$\qquad = \dfrac{5.88}{\sqrt{114}}$

$\qquad = \boxed{+0.55}$

p. 5

Additional Test: $P_F = P_m$ (Other Work)

Total Sample: $\underline{N} = 300$, $\underline{N}_F = 78$, $\underline{N}_m = 222$

Illustrations of Other Work: $\underline{N} = 131$, $\underline{n}_F = 39$, $\underline{n}_m = 92$

Note: $P$ = "big $P$", $p$ = "little $p$"

① $se_{P_F - P_m} = \sqrt{p(1-p)\left(\frac{1}{\underline{N}_F} + \frac{1}{\underline{N}_m}\right)}$ ; where $p = \dfrac{n_F + n_m}{\underline{N}_F + \underline{N}_m}$

$= \sqrt{.4367(.5633)\left(\frac{1}{78} + \frac{1}{222}\right)}$ $\qquad = \dfrac{39 + 92}{78 + 222}$

$= .0656$ $\qquad\qquad = .4367$

② $z = \dfrac{P_F - P_m}{se_{P_F - P_m}}$ , where $P_F = \dfrac{n_F}{\underline{N}_F} = \dfrac{39}{78} = .50$

$= \dfrac{.50 - .4144}{.0656}$ $\qquad P_m = \dfrac{n_m}{\underline{N}_m} = \dfrac{92}{222} = .4144$

$= \boxed{1.31}$

③ Effect Size $\emptyset = \dfrac{z}{\sqrt{N}}$

$= \dfrac{1.31}{\sqrt{131}}$

$= \dfrac{1.31}{11.45} = \boxed{+0.11}$

# INDEX

TO THE OWNER OF THIS BOOK:

We hope that you have found *Writing Papers in Psychology,* 4th edition, useful. So that this book can be improved in a future edition, would you take the time to complete this sheet and return it? Thank you.

School and address: ⎯⎯⎯⎯⎯⎯⎯⎯⎯⎯⎯⎯⎯⎯⎯⎯⎯⎯⎯⎯⎯⎯⎯⎯⎯

Department: ⎯⎯⎯⎯⎯⎯⎯⎯⎯⎯⎯⎯⎯⎯⎯⎯⎯⎯⎯⎯⎯⎯⎯⎯⎯⎯⎯⎯⎯⎯⎯

Instructor's name: ⎯⎯⎯⎯⎯⎯⎯⎯⎯⎯⎯⎯⎯⎯⎯⎯⎯⎯⎯⎯⎯⎯⎯⎯⎯⎯⎯

1. What I like most about this book is: ⎯⎯⎯⎯⎯⎯⎯⎯⎯⎯⎯⎯⎯⎯

⎯⎯⎯⎯⎯⎯⎯⎯⎯⎯⎯⎯⎯⎯⎯⎯⎯⎯⎯⎯⎯⎯⎯⎯⎯⎯⎯⎯⎯⎯⎯⎯⎯⎯⎯⎯⎯

⎯⎯⎯⎯⎯⎯⎯⎯⎯⎯⎯⎯⎯⎯⎯⎯⎯⎯⎯⎯⎯⎯⎯⎯⎯⎯⎯⎯⎯⎯⎯⎯⎯⎯⎯⎯⎯

2. What I like least about this book is: ⎯⎯⎯⎯⎯⎯⎯⎯⎯⎯⎯⎯⎯⎯⎯

⎯⎯⎯⎯⎯⎯⎯⎯⎯⎯⎯⎯⎯⎯⎯⎯⎯⎯⎯⎯⎯⎯⎯⎯⎯⎯⎯⎯⎯⎯⎯⎯⎯⎯⎯⎯⎯

⎯⎯⎯⎯⎯⎯⎯⎯⎯⎯⎯⎯⎯⎯⎯⎯⎯⎯⎯⎯⎯⎯⎯⎯⎯⎯⎯⎯⎯⎯⎯⎯⎯⎯⎯⎯⎯

3. My general reaction to this book is: ⎯⎯⎯⎯⎯⎯⎯⎯⎯⎯⎯⎯⎯⎯⎯

⎯⎯⎯⎯⎯⎯⎯⎯⎯⎯⎯⎯⎯⎯⎯⎯⎯⎯⎯⎯⎯⎯⎯⎯⎯⎯⎯⎯⎯⎯⎯⎯⎯⎯⎯⎯⎯

4. The name of the course in which I used this book is: ⎯⎯⎯⎯⎯

⎯⎯⎯⎯⎯⎯⎯⎯⎯⎯⎯⎯⎯⎯⎯⎯⎯⎯⎯⎯⎯⎯⎯⎯⎯⎯⎯⎯⎯⎯⎯⎯⎯⎯⎯⎯⎯

5. Were all of the chapters of the book assigned for you to read? ⎯⎯⎯⎯⎯

   If not, which ones weren't? ⎯⎯⎯⎯⎯⎯⎯⎯⎯⎯⎯⎯⎯⎯⎯⎯⎯⎯⎯⎯

6. In the space below, or on a separate sheet of paper, please write specific suggestions for improving this book and anything else you'd care to share about your experience in using the book.

⎯⎯⎯⎯⎯⎯⎯⎯⎯⎯⎯⎯⎯⎯⎯⎯⎯⎯⎯⎯⎯⎯⎯⎯⎯⎯⎯⎯⎯⎯⎯⎯⎯⎯⎯⎯⎯

⎯⎯⎯⎯⎯⎯⎯⎯⎯⎯⎯⎯⎯⎯⎯⎯⎯⎯⎯⎯⎯⎯⎯⎯⎯⎯⎯⎯⎯⎯⎯⎯⎯⎯⎯⎯⎯

⎯⎯⎯⎯⎯⎯⎯⎯⎯⎯⎯⎯⎯⎯⎯⎯⎯⎯⎯⎯⎯⎯⎯⎯⎯⎯⎯⎯⎯⎯⎯⎯⎯⎯⎯⎯⎯

⎯⎯⎯⎯⎯⎯⎯⎯⎯⎯⎯⎯⎯⎯⎯⎯⎯⎯⎯⎯⎯⎯⎯⎯⎯⎯⎯⎯⎯⎯⎯⎯⎯⎯⎯⎯⎯

Optional:

Your name: _____ Date: _____

May Brooks/Cole quote you, either in promotion for *Writing Papers in Psychology*, 4th edition, or in future publishing ventures?

   Yes: _____ No: _____

   Sincerely,

   *Ralph and Mimi Rosnow*